T0021374

SAVED FROM ADDICTION

How Faith in Jesus Changed My Life

BY
CHAD T. YOUNG

WESTBOW PRESS®
A DIVISION OF THOMAS NELSON & ZONDERVAN

WestBow Press books may be ordered through booksellers or by contacting:

WestBow Press
A Division of Thomas Nelson & Zondervan
1663 Liberty Drive
Bloomington, IN 47403
www.westbowpress.com
1 (866) 928-1240

ISBN: 978-1-5127-5733-0 (sc)
ISBN: 978-1-5127-5734-7 (hc)
ISBN: 978-1-5127-5732-3 (e)

Library of Congress Control Number: 2016915604

Print information available on the last page.

WestBow Press rev. date: 10/17/2016

Give praise to the Lord, proclaim His name; make known among the nations what He has done. (*New International Version*, 1 Chronicles 16:8)

Saved from Addiction

Thanks and Acknowledgements

To my Lord who has revealed Himself to me as an incredibly compassionate, gracious Redeemer of lost souls. Without Him there would be no testimony for me to give.

To my wife, Rene, who continues to help me grow as a husband and a father and supported me completely in writing this book. She also did a lot of proof reading for me. Most importantly, she constantly pours herself out for our family. Thanks babe for being who Christ created you to be.

To Steve Kmetz who challenged me to understand my own journey of transformation and to be a continuous student of God's will in my life.

To Krista Johnson who labored for hours helping me to edit this book and refine my writing skills. Thanks also for the encouragement and support.

Thanks to everyone who has been a part of my journey. We don't always understand God's plans for us while we are living out the moment, but I believe God has placed each of you in my life to have a positive impact on me. I can only hope that as I live out my days, I can have a positive impact on others.

Introduction

I find myself today, at 45 years old, looking back on my journey from addiction to my new life with Jesus. Not only is this journey down memory lane beneficial to me, it is also a way for me to help those who may be struggling with similar issues, or know someone who is. Writing allows me to proclaim what the Lord has done for me and it gives me great joy to glorify Him by sharing my story.

My prayer is that you will be encouraged by reading this book, no matter where you are on your faith journey. If you are in a good place in life, I hope this book helps you reflect on your own journey with Jesus and continues to grow you spiritually. If you find yourself at a crossroads in life, in a spiritual rut or worse, I can relate. I pray that you will find hope in these pages as you read about how knowing Jesus has helped me in my life. And if you don't have any relationship with Jesus today, my prayer is that you will come to choose Jesus for yourself and experience all of the blessings and freedoms that come from knowing the Lord.

CHAPTER 1

A Journey of Faith That Started in the Pit

Full of anger, self-hatred, pain and exhausted by life, I had come to the conclusion that it was time for me just to kill myself and end the suffering.

I looked around the little apartment I was in. Instead of a home, I felt like I was in a jail cell and the walls were moving in on me. Cheap furniture, the heavy smell of cigarette smoke, a TV, radio, a sixteenth of cocaine and an empty marijuana pipe were all I had left.

I had lost every job I had up to that point due to my drug and alcohol usage, but I usually found someone else to blame for my misfortune. At this point, it was my girlfriend's fault, well, ex-girlfriend now. She had the clarity to get while the getting was good.

I was angry at her, angry at my dismal place in life, and angry at myself. I had sabotaged myself again. No one could mess up my life as much as I could.

I sold drugs to keep up with my habits, plus I was lazy and didn't want to work. I ran in circles with others who only wanted easy money, easy highs, and easy… well, everything.

I was living for my own self-gratification, only it wasn't so gratifying anymore. It had turned into a chore. It was hard keeping up with the lies, always trying to dodge the police, and I kept on imploding. I'd get ahead, and then I would go on another drinking or drug binge not thinking of the consequences until they caught up with me.

How many times does a person have to mess everything up before they get it together? I knew the answer. The answer is that some never do, and at that time I felt like I was one of them. I thought my entire life was just going to continue to be one screw-up after the next.

I had started over several times. It was a long hard road that I couldn't seem to get off. The girl I was with left me for another guy. I can't say that I blame her. All I had going for me was selling just enough drugs to survive and then I was getting high on the rest. However, at this point, I screwed up bad.

I had robbed Peter to pay Paul one too many times. I used the money that I owed the pot dealer to pay the cocaine dealer and get an advance on the next round, and now I was out of pot and almost out of cocaine and had nothing to show for it. Both of these guys were going to be ticked off at me. If I were them, I would have taken me to the woodshed. I certainly deserved it.

I was tired and just wanted a way out. As was typical for me, I wanted an easy way out and the best solution I could come up with was to kill myself. I had accidentally overdosed on cocaine multiple times in my life; a few times when smoking crack and several times while shooting up. That night, I knew I had enough cocaine left to get high one last time as I killed myself.

As I began to think about death, I wondered what it was going to be like. I wondered if it was going to be like falling asleep and never waking up, or was it going to hurt? Then I wondered if there was life beyond this world. Was there a heaven? Was there a God? Was I about to meet God? If so, what would God say to me? Was He going to be ticked off at me? Would He send me to hell?

I had certainly given God a lot of ammunition to use against me. At that point, I remember telling myself it was time to get out of this hell that I called life. I remember saying a short prayer. Something like, "God, forgive me for what I'm about to do." And then I took the shot.

So how did I get to this point? How does anyone get to this point? Or maybe the better question is, how do you recover and get your life back together after getting to such a dark place in one's life?

My journey with God began with a desire to find meaning in life. No, wait. It started before that when I was at a place where the pain of life was so bad I wanted to kill myself. No, even before that. This journey began from birth, and it was just much later in life before I recognized the journey for what it truly was.

As a child, I grew up in the south moving back and forth between Mississippi and Texas. My family moved a lot when I was young. There was marriage and divorce, family conflicts and family secrets. There were also family gatherings and good times as well. Like many other families, over time family members went their way and we became scattered across the U.S. Each family pursued life the best they knew how.

My mom raised me going to church. Being a single-parent in the 80's was not easy for her, but she worked hard and did a good job. I certainly did not appreciate all her efforts, nor did I understand the things she was trying to protect me from which I interpreted as being over-bearing. I think as teenagers we often misinterpret a parent's desire to protect us, or attempts to lead us onto better paths, as a negative instead of an act of love and concern. I wish I would have been wise enough to ask good questions as a teenager. Instead, I assumed an awful lot, and I certainly thought I understood the world better than I did.

As I was saying, my mom took us (my older brother Jim, my little sister Bonnie, and myself) to church. The first memorable experience I had with God was at a Baptist Church in Plano, Texas. At the end of every service, the pastor would do an altar call and invite people who wanted to give their lives to Christ to come forward. He also invited those who were interested in becoming members of the church to come forward as well.

Sunday after Sunday we heard the message, then the altar call. It was expected. However; one Sunday it was different for me. I can't tell you what the preacher preached on or what was different that day. I remember getting an overwhelming feeling inside me that I needed to go forward to receive Jesus as my Savior. I remember being nervous, perhaps I even had a mild anxiety attack about going forward. Either way, I felt the conviction strongly enough that I knew I needed to act upon it.

To this day, I remember getting out of my seat and my mom asking me where I was going. I don't know if I said anything or not. I seem to recall motioning towards the front of the church indicating that I was going to go forward. I don't remember how old I was then, probably twelve or thirteen. But I remember that day, and I think God remembers that day too. My heart was sincere, but the truth is I did not understand as much as I probably should have.

Sometime that next week, I remember the pastor wanting to meet with me to make sure I understood what I was doing. I vaguely remember saying that Jesus died on the cross for my sins, that I was forgiven, and He was my Lord and Savior. The problem is, I knew the words to say, and the basics were correct, but I didn't fully understand. I was baptized the next Sunday and continued going to that church for a few more years.

Then came the teenage years –

The Journey Down the Slippery Slope

From the age of fifteen to sometime in my late twenties, all I could think about was girls. The 80's were a time of MTV, hair bands and having a good time was the main focus. When I was fifteen, I got my first job working at a McDonald's over by my high school. I worked because I wanted a vehicle. A vehicle meant freedom and an opportunity to go out with girls.

I had heard of kids in our school going to parties with alcohol. I heard stories of who got drunk, who smoked pot, and what girls were there. At that point in my life, I might have snuck a drink or two from an adult's beer, but I hadn't ever really started drinking. Since drinking alcohol seemed to be a normal practice by adults and my peers, I never really thought of it as being something dangerous, something that could harm a person or completely derail one's life. When I got older, and it seemed that more and more kids my age were drinking, I started doing so from time to time.

No one drinks their first drink and says to themselves, "I hope I become an alcoholic." And no one takes drugs for the first time saying to themselves, "I hope I get hooked on drugs and mess up my life." Or, "I hope I get arrested and go to jail for possession." We don't give much thought to all the negative consequences. Or if we do, we tend to minimize, justify, or rationalize why nothing bad will happen to us.

IN WHAT WAYS HAVE YOU -

Despite your moral compass, or the Word of God telling you that you should not do something...

- *Rationalized something you knew was wrong to do?*
- *Minimized wrong or harmful behaviors as not that big of a deal in comparison to other things you could be doing wrong?*
- *Justified yourself as having earned the right to do whatever you like?*

When things start going wrong, we seldom accept the responsibility for our mistakes. Many of us do just what Adam and Eve did in the Garden of Eden. We play the blame game.

Genesis 3:1-13 (New International Version) – Tells us when sin entered into God's creation.

Now the serpent was more crafty than any of the wild animals the LORD God had made. He said to the woman, "Did God really say, 'You must not eat from any tree in the garden'?"

**2 The woman said to the serpent, "We may eat fruit from the trees
in the garden, 3 but God did say, 'You must not eat fruit from the
tree that is in the middle of the garden, and you must not touch
it, or you will die.'"**

**4 "You will not certainly die," the serpent said to the woman. 5 "For
God knows that when you eat from it your eyes will be opened,
and you will be like God, knowing good and evil."**

**6 When the woman saw that the fruit of the tree was good for
food and pleasing to the eye, and also desirable for gaining
wisdom, she took some and ate it. She also gave some to her
husband, who was with her, and he ate it. 7 Then the eyes of
both of them were opened, and they realized they were naked;
so they sewed fig leaves together and made coverings for
themselves.**

**8 Then the man and his wife heard the sound of the LORD God as
he was walking in the garden in the cool of the day, and they hid
from the LORD God among the trees of the garden. 9 But the LORD
God called to the man, "Where are you?"**

**10 He answered, "I heard you in the garden, and I was afraid
because I was naked; so I hid."**

11 And he said, "Who told you that you were naked? Have you eaten from the tree that I commanded you not to eat from?"

12 The man said, "The woman you put here with me—she gave me some fruit from the tree, and I ate it."

13 Then the LORD God said to the woman, "What is this you have done?"

The woman said, "The serpent deceived me, and I ate."

Blame it on the snake, blame it on the woman, and blame it on God.

That says something about our human nature, doesn't it? Who taught Adam and Eve to avoid accepting responsibility? Who taught them to point the finger at someone else? It wasn't really a lie, but it sure was a way of avoiding responsibility. I guess we shouldn't be so surprised at ourselves. Yet, we act surprised by the foolish things we do.

"I can't believe I did that. What was I thinking? I'll learn my lesson this time," or so I said, on many occasions. Only to do a repeat performance, often times within 24 hours of making yet another empty declaration to change. I kid you not.

The first time I got arrested for possession of marijuana, I was angry. "It wasn't my fault man made these stupid laws," I rationalized. "Pot was made by God. How dare they make something illegal that God created?!" Isn't it strange how we throw in references to God whenever it supports our argument? The rest of the time I wasn't worried about what God thought about it, nor did I care. I only cared about what I wanted. Just like a big baby, me, me, me.

Anyhow, I got arrested for possession of marijuana. After I had gotten out of jail that evening I went straight to the bar and shared my story of the great injustice that had been done to me with anyone who would listen. One of those listening ears had compassion on me and offered to "burn one" with me. So we went out to his car and rolled one up and before we even got a chance to light it, a cop pulled up. He obviously knew what was going on as he had us get out of the car. He searched the car and found the joint in no time flat. Not even eight hours had gone by since I was released from jail and I was going back for a second possession of marijuana charge.

I can laugh about it now, but back then I was ticked off. Of course, I blamed it all on the stupid laws, the police for what I felt was an unlawful search, and any other reason I could think of.

Perhaps you would think this would be enough to get my attention and that I'd make some changes in my life. NOPE. I kept getting progressively worse. I added other drugs to my repertoire along with chasing after women. I was chasing anything I thought would make me feel good, or at least help me not to feel bad.

There were days when I had to drink, or smoke pot, so that I could feel "normal." I didn't feel like my day was right until I had some sort of buzz going. Whenever you use drugs as much as I did, you eventually end up selling them to try to keep up with your habits. To be quite honest, I don't know how I survived the 90's. The truth is, I almost didn't.

CHAPTER 2

God's Grace at Work Behind the Scenes

There were probably about a dozen times that I accidentally overdosed on drugs, usually cocaine. There were times the people I was using drugs with thought I was a goner, and I nearly was. There was one guy that helped bring me back on two separate occasions. I don't remember much but from what I understand, he had to pound on my chest to get me up and going again. Just about every time I overdosed I'd tell myself, "That's it, I have to stop this." But I kept going right back to it.

There was a part of me that honestly wanted to stop. During those years, I did make some sincere attempts to get my life together without drugs and alcohol. Today I jokingly (yet sincerely) say I had tried everything I knew to try. I did an outpatient program, an inpatient program; I went to AA, NA, and probably AAA. I did 90 meetings in 90 days.

I had people offer to help me. One of my roommates did his best to be a good influence on me. Even though we smoked enough pot together to get half the state of Texas high, he drew the line where I seemed to be unable to. He tried to encourage me to take up some healthy hobbies like fishing, but I wasn't biting. Strangely enough, today I love fishing and go as often as I can.

My dad helped me out on many occasions. He had a business and put me to work. Honestly, I didn't appreciate the opportunity he was giving me as much as I should have. I'd work for a while, get myself out of the mess I was in, then I would start the cycle all over again.

My brother went out of his way to try to help me, and I sincerely tried to stay on the path. Out of all the people I let down in those days, he was the one I had the most regret over. I was able to stay sober for about six months, which was longer than any time before. But boredom was setting in. I was "white knuckling" it. I didn't tell anyone how much I was thinking about using. I should have talked about it but at the time, it seemed pointless. I was bored and tired of being bored. So, hurricane Chad struck again and did so with a vengeance.

ROCK BOTTOM

Before long I sank to new lows. I don't know how many "rock bottoms" a person gets. I don't think anyone knows that answer. I thank God there can be a last rock bottom without dying. For me, rock bottom has come to have a new meaning. Probably most people see rock bottom as the worst a person can get, or that they have hit an all-time low. That is until they sink to a new low or return to an old low.

For me, rock bottom means there is an opportunity to stop the fall and start the climb upward. That "thud" of hitting rock bottom is an opportunity to knock some sense into us. The pain gets our attention and makes us question ourselves. Is this really what I want out of life? Rock bottom is like God smacking us upside the head and saying, "Wake up before it's too late!" What's amazing is that God's grace can also be, and often is, found at "rock bottom."

I'm not going to write about all my rock bottoms, all the times God smacked me upside the head trying to get my attention, I'll just say I've had plenty of them and will leave it at that. But there was one rock bottom that was different than all the rest. At that time in my life, I was deep into cocaine once again. I was robbing Peter to pay Paul with the people who were giving me drugs to sell for them, and

I had dug myself into a pretty good hole. I owed some guys money, but I had nothing to show for it, and I had no idea what I could do to make it right.

During those years, I had been suicidal on a few occasions. I had begun to think that suicide was a legitimate way to get myself out of the messy life I was living. I was angry at myself. I had let down myself and others. I lost any self-respect I had.

This particular night I was at the end of my rope. I didn't know what else to do. I couldn't see any way to fix the situation I had gotten myself into. For me, it was all hopeless. Not just the situation but I felt hopeless. Even if I could find a way to put things back together, I had been through this so many times already, I was exhausted with the thought of starting all over again. I just wanted to escape from my life. My plan was simple. I was going to overdose intentionally by taking a large shot of cocaine.

As I began to prepare myself for my final action, I began to think about death. I wondered what it was going to be like. I wondered if it was going to be like falling asleep and never waking up, or was it going to hurt? Then I wondered if there was life beyond this world. Was there a heaven? Was there a God? Was I about to meet God? If so, what would God say to me? Was He going to be ticked off at me? Would He send me to hell?

At that point, I remember telling myself that I was already living in hell, and it was time to get out of this hell that I called life. I remember saying a short prayer. Something like, "God, forgive me for what I'm about to do." And then I took the shot.

I assume that as I took that shot, I quickly took a nose dive. All I remember was that when I woke up, I was gasping for air. It was like I had been underwater too long and I was frantically gasping and panting for air. That's what it was like. I was fighting with all my might struggling to breathe. I was completely confused and disoriented. I had no idea where I was or what was going on. As I sat there catching my breath, it slowly started coming back to me.

Then it hit me like a ton of bricks, oh no, I was still alive! What in the world was I going to do now? I remember being upset with myself, thinking what a failure I was. I couldn't even kill myself the right way. I sat there for a bit and cried, feeling sorry for myself. Then my thoughts turned to God. I started talking with the Creator that night. It wasn't some deep theological prayer; it was more of a plea of desperation.

Here's what I recall. I remember saying, "God, I don't know if you are real or not. But if you are real, please do something with my life because I hate the way I am living."

JESUS MEETS US AT OUR POINT OF CRISIS – NOW THAT'S LOVE

I was just about as ungodly of a person as I could be. In Christian terms, I was a big time sinner. I was doing just about everything that the Bible says not to do. I was lost in the wilderness and was too blind to know it.

But God's love is abounding.

The Bible tells us in Romans 5:8

But God demonstrates his own love for us in this: While we were still sinners, Christ died for us.

Of course, I didn't know it at that time. That's what makes God's love so awesome to me. I had no idea that even while I was living in sin, God was pulling for me. He wasn't against me at all. I had it all wrong. I didn't realize that God's grace was at work even when I wasn't living for Him. What a generous and loving God!

Mark 2:17

On hearing this, Jesus said to them, "It is not the healthy who need a doctor, but the sick. I have not come to call the righteous, but sinners."

Isn't that awesome?

Think about the time you were at your worst. That is when God should have been the angriest at you. Instead, He went, in the person of Jesus, to the cross to shed His own blood for our sins. This was a hard concept for me to get, but once it sank in it would forever change my life.

Consider the story of the Prodigal Son – Luke 15:11-32 – just read all of Luke 15 and you'll see God's heart in seeking out the lost.

Jesus gave this parable thinking of me, and so many other people, to help us understand God's heart for sinners.

I will quickly paraphrase this story for those who are not familiar with it.

The young son of a rich man told his dad he wanted his inheritance to go away from his father and live life on his own terms. Obviously, the son wanted to live in a way that was not in line with the father's values, or else he would not have had to leave.

The dad, while heartbroken, gave his son what he asked for. The father knew if he did not allow the son to make his own decisions, that the son would always be resentful towards the father. So the father lets him go.

The young man went far away and blew his money drinking and fulfilling his lustful ways. Then he ran out of money. The country he was in was in a great depression, and the only job the son could find was feeding the pigs of a farmer. This farmer valued the son less than he valued the pigs. In fact, that farmer took better care of the pigs than he did the young man. Things were so bad the young man began to wish he was one of the pigs.

One day, the young man realized his father treated his servants far better than this. He decided he would return home and beg for his father's forgiveness and ask his father if he could work as one of his servants.

While the son was still far away, the father saw the son coming (for the father had watched for his son to return every day since he had left). The father quickly ran out to greet his son and welcomed him back home. He brought a robe and covered his son to hide his shame, gave him some sandals, and put the family ring on his finger. He welcomed him back into the family.

The father then ordered a big welcome home feast. The father wasn't mad at the son. Instead, he was thankful the son had returned. What an awesome father!

God has shown me that every rock bottom is an opportunity to start your comeback story. Rock bottom is a place where you can look up to God, and begin your journey out of the pit. God's not angry with you, just as the prodigal son's father was not mad at him. God loves us.

In the story of the prodigal son, it is understood that the father in this story represents God. The prodigal son represents all of us who are sinners. Now let me give you a deeper glimpse into the father.

While the son was out living his sinful life, the father was waiting for his son to return. Look at how he waited. He didn't wait stewing about what the son had done and practicing his lecture speech. He waited by setting aside a "best robe", sandals, the family ring, and was fattening up a calf. He had all this waiting to give to his son whenever he chose to return.

God, like the father in this story, is preparing for a celebration when you return to Him. Isn't that GREAT NEWS!?

> *If you are struggling to find your way in life I encourage you to turn to the One who can heal. Not only can God heal situations and circumstances, but He can heal your entire life.*
>
> *If you know someone who has lost their way, pray for them and encourage them to start talking to God, no matter where they are in life.*
>
> *God wants us to come to Him with our problems, anger, frustrations and desires. He wants us to own our wrongs and confess them. As we start spending more time with Him, reading His Word, the Bible, and talking to Him in prayer we grow in knowledge and understanding. See what God does for you when you draw close to Him!*

Here's a promise from God's Word, He desires this for each of us –

2 Chronicles 7:14

if my people, who are called by my name, will humble themselves and pray and seek my face and turn from their wicked ways, then I will hear from heaven, and I will forgive their sin and will heal their land.

That's what God did for me. In my pain, I cried out, and God heard me. My cry to God was the beginning of my seeking Him, my road to returning to the Father. I had to humble myself and recognize that I needed help. I needed God in my life.

I didn't really understand God, but God understood me. I didn't know God, but God knew me. For me, it was like a person drowning in a raging ocean of problems, most (if not all) of which I had created for myself. I was reaching out trying to find something, anything to cling to for dear life. At that moment, I realized there was no safety float to grab, no hand to reach for, but God's.

The very God I had mocked, run away from, and put to death from existence in my life was now the only one who could rescue me. My problems were bigger than I was and I didn't even know where to begin. It was that moment when I finally fully recognized how truly lost I was in life, and how much I needed a beacon of light to point the way.

For the prodigal son, it was the moment when he realized that the pigs were more valuable to his master than he was. Desiring to be cared for as much as the pigs was his rock bottom.

Waking up to the reality of his situation began his comeback story. Just as a failed suicide attempt would become mine. Today, I work at a men's homeless shelter helping others to overcome their struggles. I love telling the men that come to the shelter, this could be the beginning of their comeback story. The first thing they need to do is choose to come home to the Father.

CHAPTER 3

The Journey Home Begins

My journey to find God, and myself, started when I was looking for the answers in the wrong places, or perhaps refusing to look in the right places. Finding the path to move forward was a bumpy road. I didn't do any of the normal things you might think I would do. In fact, I intentionally avoided the very places that could have helped me the most. I did not start my search for God by going to church or talking to a pastor.

For some reason, I had resentments towards Christianity, the church and "those hypocritical people" who called themselves Christians. In those days, I had made a sweeping generalization and judged them all by looking at a few. I thought that if I saw flaws in their values and practices, then I could write them off. Wouldn't you know I would only look at people's shortcomings, and I would rush to judgment about them. Thus, I also rushed to judgment about Christianity.

Isn't that ironic? The main complaint I had with Christians was I thought they were judgmental hypocrites, it turns out I was one and didn't even know it. I expected Christians to be perfect and when I found they weren't I would use it as justification to shun them. I was quick to point the finger of accusation whenever there was a story of a pastor who fell to temptation, or a denomination which covered corruption within, or ... well, you get the point.

I was ready to use people's short-comings against them as if I were on the moral high-road. HA! What I wasn't seeing was that Christians are regular people who, for the most part, are trying to live life in a godly way, in an ungodly world. Just as I wasn't perfect at living by my own rules, neither were they. I had a lot to learn.

Let me just be blunt for a moment. The truth is, I'm a pretty hard-headed guy. I'm smart enough to get myself into trouble and too smart to ask for help. Isn't that ironically dumb of me?

HAVE YOU EVER JUMPED TO CONCLUSIONS ABOUT GOD OR CHRISTIANS THAT PAINTED THEM IN A NEGATIVE LIGHT? Perhaps some of you have like I did.

You know, perception is a strange thing. It makes you feel like you have a good understanding of something or that you have enough information to make a decision except it often comes in the form of a judgment. I have to admit I still wrestle with the demon of faulty perception from time to time. I'm learning as I go not to be so hasty to judge, though sometimes I still do, Lord help me.

How about you? Do you jump to the wrong conclusions from time to time? Or perhaps think everything you interpret is correct? Can someone be a good Christian and still have flaws? Or do you expect all Christians to behave perfectly? Is that a realistic expectation?

Have you ever jumped to conclusions about Jesus because of something negative you believe about Christians or the church? A public favorite I have heard is people saying they don't follow Jesus because of hypocrites in the church. What great expectations we have of how other people should behave.

Romans 3:23

For all have sinned and fall short of the glory of God

> *If only we could all humble ourselves and admit we are all sinners, both inside the church and outside the church. There are many Christians who understand this, but at the same time, we still have a long way to go.*

So, in my typical procrastinating way, I slowly started searching. Over the years, I had a lot of influence from my dad and a friend of his. They're into the new age movement. They're good people, and they have a heart for the light and a good sense that there is a spiritual battle going on. They do their best to fight for the light, as they understand it. I'm thankful for them and their journey. They helped me in many ways, some of which I still may not understand.

Please understand, I do not follow new age beliefs today. It was a phase I went through which I believe God used to bring me home to Him. However; it made me appreciate the Bible all the more. I needed certainty. The Bible is clear on what God wants from His people. I needed this clear direction in my life.

During this time, I had moved out of Houston to a small East Texas town called Buffalo. I was working for my dad, trying to do better. At the same time, I was still a long way off. In those days, better for me meant not doing cocaine. But I still drank alcohol and smoked pot. Now and then, I would have a relapse with cocaine, but my relapses were not the huge, chaotic messes they had been in the past. I wanted to quit and do right. When I fell to temptation, I was a little quicker to dust myself off and get back on the wagon.

From Heartache to a Fierce Determination to Change

A few things happened during this part of the journey that was pretty impactful on me. I got into a relationship with a girl who was fighting her own demons, which I didn't know until later. During our relationship, she shared she was pregnant. It was unclear if I was the father or not. I don't want to expose her or cast blame; I was just as much to blame for our situation as she was.

She had the option of having an abortion, but her mother, a Christian woman, urged her not to abort but rather give the child up for adoption. Thankfully, this is what she chose to do.

Here's what made the deepest impact on me.

After things had fallen apart between us, I moved to San Marcos, Texas, near some friends. One day, I got a knock on my door. I was surprised to see a Sheriff's Deputy there. To tell you the truth I was wondering if I had a warrant out for my arrest. I couldn't think of anything I had done recently that could have gotten me in trouble but with me, it was certainly a possibility.

The officer began to explain that he was serving a subpoena for me to appear in court. I was being sued for custody of the child that my ex-girlfriend was giving up for adoption. Although I firmly believed that I was not the father, the possibility that this could be my child tore me up inside.

I took a good look at myself, and I didn't like what I saw. There was a side of me that wanted to be the father and a dad. I started rationalizing to myself that maybe I could do it. Maybe I could be a single dad. Maybe I could find a way to juggle things and make it work.

The truth was I had put myself in a very bad position. My driver's license was suspended, and I had no vehicle. I was living a couple of miles outside of town and rode a bicycle to get to work. I was living week to week, hand to mouth. I was still struggling to manage my life. How was I going to take care of, and provide a good home for, this precious child?

Did I say the thought of all this tore me up inside? I was so mad at myself. I flip-flopped back and forth between my desire to accept my responsibility as a father and facing the ugly reality of my situation. It's interesting, as I look back I realize that the more I thought about this child, the less it mattered to me whether I was the child's biological father or not. I started to accept the fact that the child could be mine. Thus, I had to ask myself whether or not I was going to be up to the task of actually being a parent.

One day, I called my friend Joe and let him know I was struggling. Joe didn't know what to say. He told his wife Lila who called me and helped me work through it. She let me know she was adopted, and she was thankful for what her birth mother had done for her. She, as a mother of three kids, told me how raising a child was a huge challenge, and she honestly didn't see how I could do it in my current situation.

Lila also affirmed the emotional torment I was feeling. This torment I was feeling inside was my love for the child. She told me that if I ever got a chance to meet this child I could honestly tell her that giving up my parental rights was the hardest thing I ever had to do. But I did it because she would have a better life with the adoptive parents than what I was able to provide for her.

This gave me the kick in the pants that I needed. I promised myself that I was going to get my life together so that when I did have the opportunity to be a dad again, I would be ready and able to be the dad I wanted to be. Thank you God for answering that prayer!

Becoming Willing to Meet Jesus

Shortly after all this happened, I moved back to Buffalo to work with my dad again. However, this time was different. I didn't want to be the same man. I wanted to change, more than I ever had. It was no longer just about me being happy. I realized I was missing out on the blessings of life because I couldn't seem to get myself together.

My dad's friend, Sandee, gave me a book to read. It was on the power of positive speaking. It talked about the power of the tongue to unleash positive energy, or negative energy, by what you say. The gist of the book was that if you say good things then good things will come to you, say bad things and bad things will come to you.

What was so significant about this book for me was the fact that the author quoted the Bible as her source of authority to back up what she was teaching. She quoted Jesus as well. This book got me thinking; perhaps there was more to the Bible than I thought. For the first time in my adult life, I wanted to learn more about what the Bible had to say. I wanted to learn more about Jesus.

> *In the Gospel of John 1:43-51, Philip, after meeting Jesus, goes and finds his friend Nathaniel. And he tells Nathaniel that he believes he found the Messiah that Moses and the prophets had talked about. Philip encourages Nathaniel to come and see for himself.*
>
> *What was it that helped you to be open to Jesus? Was it a trusted friend or family member wanting to share their faith with you? Was it a testimony you heard? Was it an experience you had that you just couldn't explain?*
>
> *There is something that motivates us to open our hearts and minds to Jesus.*
>
> *Like Nathaniel, I was not going to take someone else's word for who Jesus was. I did NOT want to go to church. I did NOT want to become a Christian. I didn't want someone else to tell me about the Bible or Jesus. I had to find out for myself. I wanted to come to my own conclusions. Other people need to be given the time and opportunity to come and meet Jesus and decide for themselves what they believe about Him. Like Philip, we hope they come to see what we see in Jesus, the Messiah, and Savior of the world.*

I had the desire for the first time in my adult life to read the Bible. I didn't have a Bible at the time but I planned to get one the next time I went to a bookstore.

A few months passed but the desire to learn more about the Bible had not left me. This seed of hope was planted in me. I was looking forward to seeing what I might learn. One day, I was driving down the street and saw a bookstore. I suddenly remembered that I wanted to get a Bible so I quickly pulled in.

I asked the clerk to point me towards the Bibles. WOWser! Whoever would have thought there would be so many different types of Bibles. How in the world was I going to choose? I didn't have much money so I immediately started looking for those that cost the least. Then I saw something on one of the Bibles that I remembered from going to church as a child, it said that the letters of the Lord were in red.

So that was it. I grabbed a King James Version, red letter Bible and it was the best $8 investment I have ever made. That $8 hasn't come back a hundred-fold, it has come back a thousand-fold and still counting!!!!!

I went home and quickly opened the Bible and started thumbing through the pages. Man, was I lost and out of my element. I was looking for the letters in red. I started at the front of the book. I didn't know anything about the Bible. Everything I might have learned in Sunday school as a child had disappeared. I remembered a few stories, like Noah and the great flood, Moses and the parting of the Red Sea, and Jesus' death upon a cross, but I didn't understand them, nor did I remember where they were in the Bible.

I remember being surprised that I didn't find any letters in red until I got almost two-thirds of the way through the book. I found those red letters in the book called, *The Gospel According to Matthew*, and I started reading. That is when I met Jesus as an adult.

CHAPTER 4

Beginnings – The Alpha

Before I was able to come to any conclusions on who Jesus was, I needed to work out some issues regarding my questions about God. Was I willing to be open to what the Bible was going to teach me about God?

Genesis 1:1

In the beginning, God created the heavens and the earth.

John 1

1 In the beginning was the Word, and the Word was with God, and
the Word was God. [2] He was with God in the beginning. [3] Through
him all things were made; without him nothing was made that
has been made. [4] In him was life, and that life was the light of all
mankind.

Revelation 22:13

I am the Alpha and the Omega, the First and the Last, the Beginning and the End.

God created us.

I don't want to try to argue things I don't fully understand. I don't understand the mechanics of how everything came together the way it did for us to have life as we know it. But there does seem to be a lot of evidence of an Intelligent Design in the universe, our world, plants, animals, and humanity. For some, this is a philosophical debate, for others a theological debate, and for some a scientific debate. Regardless of what area a person argues from, they are always left to defend their theory of life coming into existence versus the biblical view. This was something I had to wrestle with too as I began believing in God, the Bible, and Jesus.

William Paley, an 18th-century clergyman and philosopher, used a widely argued analogy stating that if one were to find a watch in the wilderness, then one could assume there was a watchmaker. The premise is simple. The inner workings of a watch show various gears and springs put together in such a way that they could not have come together by accident. It's too complex to be an accident of nature. Therefore, there must be a Watchmaker, even though we may not see such a person.

Consider our universe and our world as a giant jigsaw puzzle. If one embraces the big bang theory (that all the universe came into existence as the result of an explosion billions of years ago), then the conclusion is that these millions of puzzle pieces went flying through the universe and put themselves together without any specific reason or purpose. Not only that, but in such a uniquely organized way that this event created everything we know and see. Most miraculously of all, this celestial explosion somehow also created life.

If I were to open a puzzle box and throw the pieces into the air how many times do you think I would have to do that before the puzzle pieces put themselves together? I would argue that even if the puzzle only had fifty pieces, the odds of the puzzle pieces coming together during a free-fall without a hand guiding them is virtually impossible.

To suggest the pieces of the universe could fall into place on their own, without an outside intelligent force putting the puzzle pieces together, seems to be a bigger leap of faith than faith in God having His hand or in this case, His Word, involved in it.

Here we are, living on a round earth, spinning at the rate of about 1,040 miles per hour (not speeding up or slowing down, but consistently moving). We orbit around the sun at the speed of 67,000 miles per hour. Gravity (which to me has a specific, designed purpose) and laws of physics all come together in an intelligently organized fashion to keep us going at both of those rates so that we can have a livable climate.

Plants take in carbon dioxide and release oxygen through the process of photosynthesis. Humans and animals breathe in oxygen and expel carbon dioxide. Each of us, in our normal cycle of living, benefits the other. All plants and animals seem to have a reproductive system which keeps them reproducing only their own kind, not differing types of life.

We have beautiful fields, mountain ranges, lakes, oceans, and gorgeous sunrises and sunsets, to look upon. What I began to see, that I hadn't seen before, was God's fingerprints on all of creation.

My point in sharing all this is that I was coming to terms with the reality that there had to be a God. That God was intelligent and intentional in creating the world. Thus, God must have a plan and purpose for us. I needed to find God's purpose for me.

This led me to think that if there is this intelligent God out there that created the world, and all living beings, and if He does have a purpose for us, wouldn't this intelligent God communicate to us to help us understand this life He has given us?

So it only makes sense that God would enter into His creation to help us know and understand Him and His plan for us. That's exactly what

He did throughout history in the Bible, in the Garden of Eden and in the person of Jesus Christ. Most importantly, He continues to interact with us here and now.

The Bible tells us that in Jesus, God the Father stepped down from His heavenly throne and came into the world as Jesus Christ. Here is where we get the concept of the Trinity. There is only One God. God has revealed himself to us in three different ways. God the Father is our Creator. God the Son is Jesus where God Himself lived as a human being as part of the created world. God, the Holy Spirit, is His Spirit alive and everywhere at once. God is moving in our lives through His Holy Spirit to help us and guide us through life.

I know the Trinity can be confusing so let me say it another way. I am a father of my children. I am also a son of my parents. I have different roles as a father from what I have as a son. As a son, I lived under the authority and provision of my parents. I depended on them for guidance and to teach me how to live. As a father, my role is to be a provider for my family. My job is to teach my kids how to grow up so they can live well in this world. I want my children to succeed in life, which is God the Father's desire for each of us.

In addition to being a father and a son myself, I am also a spirit being. We all are. Think about it. Who are you? Are you your body parts? No, the real you is inside your body making decisions and choosing how to interact with life. If you were to lose your legs, would you be less you? No, because at the core of who you are is a spirit inside you.

So I, made in God's image, am also a Trinitarian being. I'm a father, a son and a spirit all in one. I hope this image helps you with understanding why we say there is only One God, known in three ways. Father, Son, and Holy Spirit.

As I said earlier, I have come to understand that God wants to be known. Thus, He has made a way for us to know Him. The Bible tells us that God is love, and love must be expressed. Love desires to be in a relationship, that is, to have that love reciprocated. God has blessed us in giving us the opportunity to choose whether or not we are going to love Him.

We can choose what kind of people we are going to be. Although we are all both good and bad because of our strengths and weaknesses, we have the ability to change. We have the ability to choose whether or not we are going to seek our Creator. We have the ability to choose whether or not we are going to live in a loving relationship with the Almighty. True love does not force itself upon those it loves, but rather gives the object of its love the ability to choose if it wants to love in return.

Here's the thing: God has chosen to love you. Not because you are good or bad. But because you are His child, His creation. God asks us to love Him in return. Why? Because He wants us to find the greatest blessings in life and God, like any of us, wants to be a part of the lives of those who love Him.

When we desire to show love to someone we seek to please them, bless them, spend time with them and give them things that will bring them joy. God, who created us, shows His love for us. He provides for us. He came into the world in Jesus Christ to die for our sins. He redeemed us by sacrificing Himself. Knowing this, how do we show God that we love Him and appreciate His sacrifice?

Jesus said in John 15:9-17

9 "As the Father has loved me, so have I loved you. Now remain in
my love. 10 If you keep my commands, you will remain in my love,
just as I have kept my Father's commands and remain in his love.
11 I have told you this so that my joy may be in you and that your
joy may be complete. 12 My command is this: Love each other as I
have loved you. 13 Greater love has no one than this: to lay down
one's life for one's friends. 14 You are my friends if you do what I
command. 15 I no longer call you servants, because a servant does

not know his master's business. Instead, I have called you friends, for everything that I learned from my Father I have made known to you. [16] You did not choose me, but I chose you and appointed you so that you might go and bear fruit—fruit that will last—and so that whatever you ask in my name the Father will give you. [17] This is my command: Love each other.

God intends for our joy to be complete (vs. 11). Unfortunately, in our fallen state of humanity, we rarely receive the full joy the Lord intends for us to experience. We squander the gifts He intends to give us when we are not willing to live in harmony with Him, or follow His commands, or love one another. It's unfortunate that we, who have been so greatly blessed, trample over His intended gifts for us as if they are nothing worthwhile.

God desires what is best for us. He reveals Himself to us in the Bible so that we may clearly know and understand Him and His great love for us. He seeks to teach us through telling the story of humanity because His desire is for us to share the joy and peace of heaven with Him for all eternity.

CHAPTER 5

The Bible as God's Word and Our Rebelliousness

Psalm 119:105

Your word is a lamp for my feet, a light on my path.

Matthew 4:4

Jesus answered, "It is written: 'Man shall not live on bread alone, but on every word that comes from the mouth of God.'"

2 Timothy 3:14-17

14 But as for you, continue in what you have learned and have
become convinced of, because you know those from whom you
learned it, 15 and how from infancy you have known the Holy
Scriptures, which are able to make you wise for salvation through
faith in Christ Jesus. 16 All Scripture is God-breathed and is useful
for teaching, rebuking, correcting and training in righteousness,
17 so that the servant of God may be thoroughly equipped for
every good work.

Even in the Garden of Eden, God spoke to Adam and Eve. God shared with them how to live. God provided all they would need. Everything God created was theirs to enjoy in its natural order. God gave them one command of what not to do.

Genesis 2:15-17

**15 The LORD God took the man and put him in the Garden of Eden
to work it and take care of it. 16 And the LORD God commanded the
man, "You are free to eat from any tree in the garden; 17 but you
must not eat from the tree of the knowledge of good and evil, for
when you eat from it you will certainly die."**

At this point, there was no sin. Man lived in harmony with God, according to God's will and design. We know that God created a woman and intended for Adam and Eve to be a mutual blessing to one another.

Here is where everything changed in the course of humanity. The serpent, the devil in disguise, began speaking to Eve questioning the faithfulness of God's Word to them.

Genesis 3:1-7

Now the serpent was more crafty than any of the wild animals the LORD God had made. He said to the woman, "Did God really say, 'You must not eat from any tree in the garden'?"

**2 The woman said to the serpent, "We may eat fruit from the trees
in the garden, 3 but God did say, 'You must not eat fruit from the
tree that is in the middle of the garden, and you must not touch
it, or you will die.'"**

**4 "You will not certainly die," the serpent said to the woman. 5 "For
God knows that when you eat from it your eyes will be opened,
and you will be like God, knowing good and evil."**

**6 When the woman saw that the fruit of the tree was good for food
and pleasing to the eye, and also desirable for gaining wisdom,
she took some and ate it. She also gave some to her husband, who
was with her, and he ate it. 7 Then the eyes of both of them were**

opened, and they realized they were naked; so they sewed fig leaves together and made coverings for themselves.

The temptation that came upon Eve was two-fold. First, was doubt of God's Word. Second, was the temptation to be like God, judging what is good and evil.

In J. Keith Miller's book, *A Hunger for Healing*, he talks about sin in two ways. There is "Sin" with a capital "S" and "sin" with a lowercase "s"[1].

Sin with a capital "S" is putting something else on the throne of your life where God is designed to live. So the capital "S" sin, the first sin, is when we kick God off the throne and put a substitute in God's place. The substitute can be yourself, another person, an object, a self-fulfilling interest or anything else.

In the case of Eve, she allowed the serpent to challenge God's authority in her life. She ousts God from the throne and places her trust in the words of the serpent. This was Sin with the capital S. The devil, being the clever liar he is, used the temptation and lure of telling Eve that she could sit on the throne and decide for herself what good and evil is. She could rule her world. She desired to sit on God's throne herself.

You were created by God, to live with God in your life guiding you. When you live your life this way, you will learn the lessons God desires you to learn and fulfill whatever meaningful purpose God intends for your life. Creation works best when it follows the design of the Creator.

Sin with the lower case "s" represents the things we do because God is not on the throne of our lives. Lie, cheat, steal, display anger, being unwilling to forgive and so on. The point is, if we truly live with God on the throne of our lives and submit to His Lordship, we would not sin at all.

---

[1] Miller, J. Keith. *A Hunger for Healing: The Twelve Steps As A Classic Model For Christian Spiritual Growth*. New York: HarperCollins Publishers. 1991, pg 3.

For example, when I have God on the throne of my life and I see a woman who is immodestly dressed, I will turn my head instead of undressing her with my mind. I give this temptation to the Lord and He helps me do the right thing. If I am to surrender to the Lordship of God and what He declares is good and evil, then I have to ask myself what God's Word says.

Matthew 5:27-28

27 "You have heard that it was said, 'You shall not commit adultery.' 28 But I tell you that anyone who looks at a woman lustfully has already committed adultery with her in his heart.

So, if at that moment I choose to give in to temptation, then I have temporarily ousted God from the throne and placed my sexual desires on the throne. Then I desire to act on my more carnal desires.

Here is the reality of what I am saying, I do my best to keep God on the throne. That is what I need to guard the most. Am I giving God's Word the proper place of authority over my life? The struggle we have with sin is we often want to live on a different set of terms than what God's Word gives us.

Romans 7:14-25

14 We know that the law is spiritual; but I am unspiritual, sold as a slave to sin. 15 I do not understand what I do. For what I want to do I do not do, but what I hate I do. 16 And if I do what I do not want to do, I agree that the law is good. 17 As it is, it is no longer I myself who do it, but it is sin living in me. 18 For I know that good itself does not dwell in me, that is, in my sinful nature. For I have the desire to do what is good, but I cannot carry it out. 19 For I do not do the good I want to do, but the evil I do not want to do—this I keep on doing. 20 Now if I do what I do not want to do, it is no longer I who do it, but it is sin living in me that does it.

**21 So I find this law at work: Although I want to do good, evil is
right there with me. 22 For in my inner being I delight in God's
law; 23 but I see another law at work in me, waging war against
the law of my mind and making me a prisoner of the law of sin at
work within me. 24 What a wretched man I am! Who will rescue
me from this body that is subject to death? 25 Thanks be to God,
who delivers me through Jesus Christ our Lord! So then, I myself
in my mind am a slave to God's law, but in my sinful nature a slave
to the law of sin.**

Sin comes as a result of the absence of God's authority being active in our lives. The byproduct of sin is death.

Romans 6:23

For the wages of sin is death,

When Adam and Eve sinned against God and ate of the Tree of Knowledge of Good and Evil, the aging process began and they started the journey towards death.

Sin produces the chaos and pain that we experience in the world today. Because humanity has determined that we want to usurp God's authority and bestow it upon ourselves, we have created the world we live in today in our own sinful, fallen image rather than reflecting the loving God who created us.

We cannot continue to blame God for the woes of the world and at the same time disregard the Word of God. Some say that God does not exist, and they use the evidence of the pain and chaos in the world as evidence without considering who is really at fault. Did God make all of our decisions for us, or have we as humanity chosen this for ourselves?

If I were to touch a burning hot stove and get burned, should I blame God? When someone murders someone else, should we blame God?

When people, out of greed steal, kill and destroy for their personal gain whom should we blame? I say it is the people themselves who choose to do this.

Didn't Eve eat the fruit of the Tree of Knowledge of Good and Evil? Didn't Adam eat of it? Haven't you and I, figuratively speaking, eaten of it? By practice, we have chosen to live outside of the Word and will of God. We all have at some point or another. We have made this world into our fallen image. This world is what it is because we have given in to our sinful nature and have not valued the Word of God as we ought to.

The condition of the sinful side of humanity is that we want to place ourselves on the throne of God. We want to judge God and each other. We want to assign what is morally right and wrong.

If one person says Action A is good and another person says Action A is bad, according to moral relativism, they are both correct. Moral relativism breeds chaos. A multitude of people acting on varying sets of rules and guidelines and telling one another which rules and guidelines for living they need to adopt. In short, if we all try to play God by judging what is good and bad, then all we have done is create chaos and judgmentalism. We begin to tear one another apart to get the other person to conform.

WE NEED GOD'S WORD TO REIGN. We need God, and only God, to be God. We need to surrender the kingdoms we are trying to build and lay our crowns down at the feet of Jesus. Then we will come to know what true peace is. Now, more than ever, we need the Absolute Truth that comes from God, that is written in the Bible, and that was lived out in the person of Jesus Christ.

Because of the chaos of "many truths that are not true" God, in His desire to help us, spoke to men throughout history. He asked them to write down His "Truth" for humanity's sake. In doing so, God has shown us the path to find our way back to Him and back into harmony with His Kingdom.

The Bible came into existence as God worked in harmony with men whose hearts were open and willing to be an instrument for God to use. Those men were not perfect, but God can use even broken vessels like us.

The challenge we have is to stop listening to the words of doubt, distrust and personal preference that are prevalent in the world today. It's time for us to turn down the noise of the world and focus on the Word of God. We can't just sit near the Word of God, or just hear the Word of God, we have to be committed to following it. We must humble ourselves because we all, even those of us who call ourselves Christians, have difficulty living out God's will.

God's Word, the Bible, is a gift to us. God's Word is here to be a light in a dark world, giving us guidance and leading each of us on a journey with our Maker. Your life will become fuller and richer. You will grow in understanding and God will use you to be a blessing to others in the world. You will be blessed while you faithfully go on the journey back to Him.

CHAPTER 6

Meeting Jesus, "Come, Follow Me."

As I started reading, aside from trying to understand some of the old language of the King James Version (all the: thee, thine, thy, thou, etc.), Jesus was usually pretty straightforward and easy to understand. Did I understand all of it, NO! Not by a long-shot. I found a lot of the Old Testament and the Epistles in the New Testament pretty confusing at first. But I stuck with it. The longer I kept reading and asking God to help me to understand, the more I eventually understood.

For me, it was kind of like putting together a giant puzzle. When I start a puzzle, I either start with the edges or with an object within the puzzle that stands out the most. This gives me a frame of reference to start seeing how the different pieces go together. At that time God was my puzzle, the Bible was the puzzle pieces, Jesus was the object for me to study to give me a better frame of reference. Learning to understand Jesus eventually helped me understand the whole Bible better.

My advice for those new to the Bible or Christianity is to start by learning about Jesus. I started with the Gospel According to Matthew, then continued reading the Gospel According to Mark, then Luke, and finally John.

At first, I was a little confused by some of the differences and similarities between these four books of the Bible. A helpful tip is to know that you are reading accounts by four separate people who wrote about the life, ministry, death and resurrection of Jesus. Each person tells their story as they remember it or based upon testimonies they heard from others.

DEVELOPING AN ADMIRATION FOR JESUS

One of the first things I loved about Jesus was how he put the chief priests and other religious leaders of the day in their place. That's kind of where I was with "organized religion" at the time. Jesus pointed out and even called them out directly, letting them know they were hypocrites.

For some reason, this helped me be more willing to read and try to understand more about Jesus. Jesus seemed like someone I'd talk to. I love the fact that he hung out with the sinners, rather than the saints. He cared about people that others in society didn't want to have anything to do with. I started admiring Jesus for his backbone in standing up to the religious elite of the day and the authenticity of his ministry to the needy.

So that was my first impression of him, one of admiration.

The Role of Skepticism

However; I have to admit I also had a lot of skepticism. I certainly didn't understand the Son of God or the references to being God in the flesh. That was a little too much for me at that time. The miracles were intriguing to me, but hard to swallow. I did admire Jesus and out of admiration, I continued reading.

There was something else about Jesus. There seemed to be an authenticity and authority, something about his teachings connected with me. I couldn't help thinking and feeling that Jesus had it right. It was like Jesus was teaching me all these little nuggets of truth. As I read more it was as if these little light bulbs were being turned on in my head for the first time, one by one.

I remember feeling a sense of conflict rising in me. On the one hand, I was looking for answers to life and Jesus seemed to have those answers in spades. But the things the Bible said He did, and the proclamations that both He and others made about who He was, well, I just had a hard time believing.

So here I was, this closet fan of Jesus. Still living in many of my sinful ways, but feeling challenged to make some changes, which I did. I wanted a new life, but I wasn't quite ready to commit. I still had too many unanswered questions. I'm sure the devil was feeding me questions and doing his best job to keep me confused. The devil certainly threw a lot of temptations my way.

Ultimately it came down to this, if I was going to make a move and be a true follower of Jesus, I was going to have to make some pretty radical changes in how I lived my life. I have to admit, that scared me. I had no idea how these changes would affect me. How would that affect my friendship with others? Where was this journey going to take me? I have to admit, I was a little scared.

Matthew 6:33 - But seek first His (God's) kingdom and His righteousness, and all these things will be given to you as well.

For months on end I continued reading the Bible trying to make sense of it all, trying to come to some conclusion.

I remember taking comfort in the fact that even the disciples, who were right there with Jesus, didn't always seem to get it. They struggled to understand Him, and they were right there with Him. But their stories of leaving all they had to follow Jesus challenged me.

Matthew 4:20 - At once they left their nets and followed Him.

Holy moly! I can't imagine what it was about Jesus at the moment when He approached them and said, "Come, follow me," that prompted them to do it. I was a bit in awe of them. What courage it must have taken for them to tell their families, "Hey we just met this guy named Jesus. He asked us to follow Him, so we are going to give up our fishing business, our boat, and our nets, and we are going to walk away from life as we know it and see where this guy takes us."

I can't imagine what their friends and family must have said to them. They must have thought they had spent too much time in the sun and were delusional. Or maybe that's just how I was feeling at the time.

Those words, "Come follow me", were haunting me. Challenging me. Beckoning me.

Jesus was challenging me personally, to draw closer to Him. To walk closer with Him. To seek to truly understand Him. Jesus, through the Bible, was speaking to me directly and inviting me to go on the journey of a lifetime with Him.

What would it cost? At that time, it felt like it would cost me everything I had ever known. It would call me to leave a lifestyle that I had embraced for so long, even though it left me physically, mentally, emotionally and spiritually wounded. How would it affect my relationships with my friends that were living lifestyles that I knew, in my heart, Jesus would not approve of?

You would think that with the dissatisfaction I had with myself and my life at that time, I would have gladly left it all behind to see where this might take me. But for some reason, probably that thing about me being so hard-headed, I just couldn't fully commit.

I did, however, continue to read the Bible. Over time, I found myself praying more and more. I remember praying for God to give me understanding. At the time I prayed it, I didn't know it was one of the prayers God promised he would answer.

James 1:5 - If any of you lacks wisdom, you should ask God, who gives generously to all without finding fault, and it will be given to you.

I should have read the next few verses but for some reason, those didn't stick out to me at the time.

James 1:6-8 - But when you ask, you must believe and not doubt, because the one who doubts is like a wave of the sea, blown and tossed by the wind. That person should not expect to receive anything from the Lord. Such a person is double-minded and unstable in all they do.

Boy was I unstable. Even worse, I was still double-minded.

My admiration for Jesus was growing. I had unwittingly gone from being an admirer of Jesus to being a student of Jesus. In some ways, I was like the disciples and didn't realize it. I was trying to understand His teachings and grasp what He was saying, but I was having a hard time putting it all together. Look at how many times the disciples did the same thing.

Matthew 19:5-12 - [5] When they went across the lake, the disciples forgot to take bread. [6] "Be careful," Jesus said to them. "Be on your guard against the yeast of the Pharisees and Sadducees."

[7] They discussed this among themselves and said, "It is because we didn't bring any bread."

[8] Aware of their discussion, Jesus asked, "You of little faith, why are you talking among yourselves about having no bread? [9] Do you still not understand? Don't you remember the five loaves for the five thousand, and how many basketfuls you gathered? [10] Or the seven loaves for the four thousand, and how many basketfuls you gathered? [11] How is it you don't understand that I was not talking to you about bread? But be on your guard against the

yeast of the Pharisees and Sadducees." [12] Then they understood that he was not telling them to guard against the yeast used in bread, but against the teaching of the Pharisees and Sadducees.

Mark 4 – Parable of the Sower

[13] Then Jesus said to them, "Don't you understand this parable? How then will you understand any parable?

After Jesus told his disciples for the second time of his coming crucifixion we read:

Mark 9:32 - But they did not understand what he meant and were afraid to ask him about it.

Even Mary and Joseph, Jesus' earthly parents, (who were spoken to by angels none the less) had difficulty understanding. Twelve years after His birth, they went looking for Jesus and found Him in the temple.

Luke 2:49-50 - [49] "Why were you searching for me?" he asked. "Didn't you know I had to be in my Father's house?" [50] But they did not understand what he was saying to them.

Nicodemus, a Pharisee (a sect of Jews well educated on the Hebrew Scriptures) and a member of the Jewish ruling council, came to Jesus struggling to understand.

John 3:9-10 - [9] "How can this be?" Nicodemus asked.

[10] "You are Israel's teacher," said Jesus, "and do you not understand these things?

Even after Jesus crucifixion and resurrection He had to teach, and correct, His disciples.

Luke 24:9-12 [9] When they came back from the tomb, they told all these things to the Eleven and to all the others. [10] It was Mary Magdalene, Joanna, Mary the mother of James, and the others with them who told this to the apostles. [11] But they did not believe the women, because their words seemed to them like nonsense.[12] Peter, however, got up and ran to the tomb. Bending over, he saw the strips of linen lying by themselves, and he went away, wondering to himself what had happened.

My point is that most of us have struggled to understand the Bible. God's Word is deep and at times complex, while at other times straightforward and simple. The challenge is to keep on reading. Keep on following Jesus and continue to ask questions and seek to understand. Just as the disciples struggled to understand everything He taught, we will too. But some good news is at the end they did comprehend and did some pretty amazing things with God.

There is an amazing adventure for those of us who are willing to surrender our lives to Him and seek to live out His will for our lives. I believe what God has done in my life is nothing short of a miracle. God now has me on the adventure of a lifetime. He's called me to live life for Him by helping others in this world. There is truly nothing as rewarding as this adventure with God.

CHAPTER 7

Jesus, The Disciples, and The Bible on Trial

My heart and mind were still unsettled about who Jesus was. I had not fully committed to Him. I was getting to know Jesus and that was good, but at the same time, I was putting Jesus on a trial of my own. I didn't realize this was what I was doing. I thought I was just doing some good critical thinking.

The truth is I was putting Jesus on trial and I was the judge who chose which evidence was admissible and which was not. I was the attorney making the arguments and I was the jury making the final decision.

I believe many, if not most of us, have put Jesus on trial at some point in our lives. Perhaps we are supposed to put Jesus on trial in order to have a faith that is our own. By this I mean, once we walk through the process of asking questions, seeking answers and coming to a conclusion our decision is firm because we have sifted through the muck and mire. Perhaps sometimes we even reach a verdict at one point in our lives and later go back with "new evidence" and put Jesus back on trial again.

Jesus, loving us, endures all the trials He is put on, over and over, by the very people He loves and longs to bless.

The trial is us asking who Jesus is. Is he just a teacher whose followers embellished great stories about Him? If that's so, then His followers (the original disciples and as well as others) are a bunch of liars to go around telling everyone that Jesus was resurrected from the grave. However, that argument really can't stand too much poking and prodding. If I were to believe Jesus' followers were a bunch of liars trying to save face after Jesus' death, there are a few things I am going to have to reconcile.

1. If they were liars, they were the most committed liars the world has ever known.
2. If they were trying to save face, they did not seem to care too much about presenting themselves in a better manner.

When Jesus was arrested in the Garden of Gethsemane, according to the Gospels of Matthew, Mark, and Luke, the disciples took off to save their own hides. Yet, after Jesus' death and burial, these men suddenly find the courage to proclaim that Jesus was the Messiah. That alone would have been bold enough yet they profess something even greater, that Jesus himself came out of the tomb on the third day after His death. He arose from the grave and appeared to them and many others, He even spoke to them.

Now come on, they surely could have come up with something more believable than that. I mean, if I was going to make something up I would have gone with something more plausible such as an angel coming down from heaven to speak to me. Or perhaps, one of the prophets had spoken to me. Or that God had given me a vision in a dream.

But no, these guys come out with Jesus is alive. He was dead, buried, and has risen! At this time in my life I was like the disciple Thomas who doubted this story. This was one of those proclamations that I, and many others, have had a hard time believing.

John 20:24-29

[24] Now Thomas (also known as Didymus), one of the Twelve, was not with the disciples when Jesus came. [25] So the other disciples told him, "We have seen the Lord!"

But he said to them, "Unless I see the nail marks in his hands and put my finger where the nails were, and put my hand into his side, I will not believe."

**26 A week later his disciples were in the house again, and Thomas
was with them. Though the doors were locked, Jesus came and
stood among them and said, "Peace be with you!" 27 Then he said
to Thomas, "Put your finger here; see my hands. Reach out your
hand and put it into my side. Stop doubting and believe."**

28 Thomas said to him, "My Lord and my God!"

**29 Then Jesus told him, "Because you have seen me, you have
believed; blessed are those who have not seen and yet have
believed."**

Verse 29 convicted me. Like doubting Thomas, I was too practical just to believe.

I've always considered myself to be fairly intelligent, though I certainly made a lot of stupid decisions in my life. One day, a preacher on TV challenged my thinking about who Jesus was and whether the stories about him could be true.

At that time in my life, I was still not going to church, but trying to find ways of understanding. TV was a great medium because it was private, meaning no one saw me going to church. I didn't have to talk to anyone, and I didn't have to feel like I was being pressured into something.

As I was listening to this preacher, he talked about the trustworthiness of the testimony of the disciples. He explained how the disciples all fled when Jesus was arrested, yet they suddenly gained a lot of backbone and lost all fear of persecution after Jesus' death.

There had to have been something that caused this change in them. The thing that caused this change must have been the resurrection. I can tell you this much, if I was there to witness Jesus' death and burial and then days later saw and spoke to Jesus in the presence of others, I think I would be thoroughly convinced.

I don't remember all the details the pastor shared. I can't even remember which pastor it was, but he started talking about the ministry, persecution and martyrdom of the disciples. How even in the face of death, when they were asked to recant their story of Jesus' resurrection, NONE of them did. If they were liars, they sure were a committed group of liars.

I might be able to understand if they had all been in a group together when they were asked to recant which might have given them courage, but that isn't how the facts unfolded. Even in the face of ridicule, abuse, imprisonment and death each man made a stand independently of the others.

Depending on whose version of events you read, you will find different accounts of which of the disciples were martyred for proclaiming Jesus' death, burial, and resurrection. I want to share with you what I've learned about the death of some of these disciples. Before I do, there is one thing I feel should be put on the table first.

I read an article on the death of the disciples, *The Death of the Twelve Apostles: How Their Martyrdom Evidences Easter* by C. Michael Patton (Patterson). This author does a good job of trying to be even-handed in his review of their deaths. He tries to give full disclosure and even grades what he considers to be the trustworthiness, or the reliability, of the accounts.

However; he makes a point in his article that should be considered. People are willing to die for what they believe in, and they have done so throughout history. Think about all our faithful soldiers who put themselves in harm's way to protect our freedoms.

Now, let's look at the negative side of this thought. People die for things they believe in, for causes they believe in. However, people can also be deceived about some of the causes they are fighting for. Mr. Patton puts on the table that jihadists kill in the name of Allah and take their lives for the cause they believe in. Just because someone is willing to die for something does not make it true.

Here's where Mr. Patton rightly discerns the difference. Whether it be one of our noble soldiers or someone we believe to be completely in the wrong, like a Muslim extremist, they are willing to fight and die for what they BELIEVE is the TRUTH. My sincerest apologies for putting the brave men and women of our armed forces in the same context as Muslim extremists. I hope everyone reading understands my intent is to show that some people fight and die for things that are the right things and some people fight and die for the wrong things. I hold our service men and women in high regard for the sacrifices they make.

The point the author makes is that the disciples are not dying for something they know to be a lie. If they were lying about Jesus' resurrection, then they would have been investing all of their life and even their death, in a known lie. Either the disciples made it up and thus are lying, or it really happened. No one in their right mind would go to the extreme of dying a torturous death for a known lie. One crazy person here and there that I could get. But all of them, defending this highly improbable position if it were not even true, that is pretty hard to imagine.

Depending on how you count them, and which sources you conclude are reliable accounts, some say all but the Apostle John died as a martyr for proclaiming Jesus Christ was the resurrected Lord. Others say eight of the thirteen died as martyrs. You may be asking how we got to thirteen disciples instead of the traditional twelve.

After Judas Iscariot had killed himself from the guilt of betraying Jesus, he was replaced by Matthias (Acts 1:26). That brings the number from eleven potential disciples back to twelve. Number thirteen would then be the Apostle Paul, whose personal encounter with the resurrected Lord Jesus Christ (Acts 9 – Paul at that time was still referred to as Saul or Saul of Tarsus) was his conversion point from hunting Christians down to raising new Christians up. I was tempted to count up to fourteen and include Stephen, the first martyr (Acts 7 – 8:2), for his testimony and bold witnessing to others of Jesus.

So here I was in my journey, being challenged to make decisions about who Jesus is. This is the trial I was putting Jesus on. Was I going to believe in Him? Was I going to believe that He was who He said He was?

Who Jesus said He was

John 14:6-9

6 Jesus answered, "I am the way and the truth and the life. No one comes to the Father except through me. 7 If you really know me, you will know my Father as well. From now on, you do know him and have seen him."

8 Philip said, "Lord, show us the Father and that will be enough for us."

9 Jesus answered: "Don't you know me, Philip, even after I have been among you such a long time? Anyone who has seen me has seen the Father. How can you say, 'Show us the Father'?

Who did the disciples say Jesus was?

Matthew 16:13-18

13 When Jesus came to the region of Caesarea Philippi, he asked his disciples, "Who do people say the Son of Man is?"

[14] They replied, "Some say John the Baptist; others say Elijah; and still others, Jeremiah or one of the prophets."

[15] "But what about you?" he asked. "Who do you say I am?"

[16] Simon Peter answered, "You are the Messiah, the Son of the living God."

[17] Jesus replied, "Blessed are you, Simon son of Jonah, for this was not revealed to you by flesh and blood, but by my Father in heaven. [18] And I tell you that you are Peter, and on this rock I will build my church, and the gates of Hades will not overcome it.

Who do you say I am?

That's the real question. Who do you say Jesus is? This question is the essence of Jesus' trial and the trials of the disciples and for us. We, in this day and age, are always putting Jesus on trial.

I understood that Jesus was not asking just His twelve disciples who they said He was. Jesus is also asking you and me, "Who do you say I am?"

Here is an interesting note: In Jesus' trial, He had all matter of false accusations made against Him. While we know Jesus to be bold in confronting the religious leaders of his day, during His trial He did not answer them except for one answer.

Matthew 26:59-64

The chief priests and the whole Sanhedrin were looking for false evidence against Jesus so that they could put him to death. [60] But they did not find any, though many false witnesses came forward.

Finally two came forward [61] and declared, "This fellow said, 'I am able to destroy the temple of God and rebuild it in three days.'"

[62] Then the high priest stood up and said to Jesus, "Are you not going to answer? What is this testimony that these men are bringing against you?"[63] But Jesus remained silent.

The high priest said to him, "I charge you under oath by the living God: Tell us if you are the Messiah, the Son of God."

[64] "You have said so," Jesus replied. "But I say to all of you: From now on you will see the Son of Man sitting at the right hand of the Mighty One and coming on the clouds of heaven."

In His trial, Jesus' only response, was that He was the Messiah, the Son of God, who will sit at the right hand of God. For them, that was more than enough to put Him to death, because they had already judged in their hearts He was not.

There is something powerful about this moment. I did not understand it right away but a couple of years later the Lord revealed something to me.

Let's look at the story of Jesus' trial with Pontius Pilate.

Matthew 27:11-26

[11] Meanwhile Jesus stood before the governor, and the governor asked him, "Are you the king of the Jews?"

"You have said so," Jesus replied.

[12] When he was accused by the chief priests and the elders, he gave no answer.[13] Then Pilate asked him, "Don't you hear the testimony they are bringing against you?" [14] But Jesus made no

**reply, not even to a single charge—to the great amazement of the
governor.**

**15 Now it was the governor's custom at the festival to release a
prisoner chosen by the crowd. 16 At that time they had a well-
known prisoner whose name was Jesus Barabbas. 17 So when the
crowd had gathered, Pilate asked them, "Which one do you want
me to release to you: Jesus Barabbas, or Jesus who is called the
Messiah?" 18 For he knew it was out of self-interest that they had
handed Jesus over to him.**

**19 While Pilate was sitting on the judge's seat, his wife sent him
this message: "Don't have anything to do with that innocent man,
for I have suffered a great deal today in a dream because of him."**

**20 But the chief priests and the elders persuaded the crowd to ask
for Barabbas and to have Jesus executed.**

**21 "Which of the two do you want me to release to you?" asked the
governor.**

"Barabbas," they answered.

**22 "What shall I do, then, with Jesus who is called the Messiah?"
Pilate asked.**

They all answered, "Crucify him!"

23 "Why? What crime has he committed?" asked Pilate.

But they shouted all the louder, "Crucify him!"

**24 When Pilate saw that he was getting nowhere, but that instead
an uproar was starting, he took water and washed his hands in
front of the crowd. "I am innocent of this man's blood," he said.
"It is your responsibility!"**

[25] All the people answered, "His blood is on us and on our children!"

[26] Then he released Barabbas to them. But he had Jesus flogged, and handed him over to be crucified.

Note that once again, Jesus does not answer to the false accusations made against Him, the only thing He answers to is His identity. This time, King of the Jews.

Here's what I learned.

There were two men there that day. One was guilty and the other was innocent. The only testimony Jesus gave about Himself was testimony that was going to get Him killed. He claimed He was the Son of God, the King of the Jews.

The other man, Barabbas, a prisoner who was brought out that day was never questioned about his guilt. If he had been, there was more than enough evidence to convict Barabbas. Everyone knew he was guilty. Yet, that day the people killed an innocent man, Jesus, for His testimony of who He was (and is). The guilty man was set free and the innocent man paid the debt for the guilty man with His life.

That is the truth. I and every other person who is guilty of sin, have no defense that we can give when the day comes for us to stand before God and give an account of our lives. I will have nothing I can say as the devil joyfully recounts all my sins. There is only one testimony I can give that will make a difference, and that is the testimony of who Jesus is, and that He is the Holy Son of God who died for my sins.

The Bible says Barabbas, but it might as well have said Chad. Jesus did not try to save himself. He willingly died for the guilty.

Later, God showed me another lesson in this.

Vs 25 – All the people answered, "His blood is on us and on our children!"

We all ought to pray that. That Jesus' blood is on our children and us. They didn't know it when they cried out for it, but the sweetest blessing those people could ever have is to have His blood covering their sin. They were crying out for His death which would be for their benefit and that of the whole world, and they didn't even realize it.

As Jesus said, His blood was poured out for the forgiveness of our sins.

Matthew 26:28

This is my blood of the covenant, which is poured out for many for the forgiveness of sins.

Ephesians 1:7

In him we have redemption through his blood, the forgiveness of sins, in accordance with the riches of God's grace

Hebrews 9:22

In fact, the law requires that nearly everything be cleansed with blood, and without the shedding of blood there is no forgiveness.

Revelation 7:14

I answered, "Sir, you know." And he said, "These are they who have come out of the great tribulation; they have washed their robes and made them white in the blood of the Lamb.

Revelation 12:11

They triumphed over him by the blood of the Lamb and by the word of their testimony; they did not love their lives so much as to shrink from death.

In the midst of the whirlwind of accusation, punishment and abuse Jesus was taking, He was keeping His composure. He was remembering that His suffering was for the benefit of those same sinners that were looking to kill Him.

CHAPTER 8

The Need for a Verdict

At this time in my life, I was still trying to come to a conclusion about Jesus. Was this true? If only I had some way of knowing for sure.

One day as I was reading the Bible, I came across a passage I had read before:

John 14:11-14

11 Believe me when I say that I am in the Father and the Father is in me; or at least believe on the evidence of the works themselves.
12 Very truly I tell you, whoever believes in me will do the works I have been doing, and they will do even greater things than these, because I am going to the Father. 13 And I will do whatever you ask in my name, so that the Father may be glorified in the Son. 14 You may ask me for anything in my name, and I will do it.

And that's when the bright idea hit. I know, I'll put this to the test and see if it is real or not.

So I set out to do what any good, red-blooded, American would do. I decided I would test Jesus, and the Bible, by doing exactly what it said. I was going to pray to God and ask for something in Jesus' name and see if God would do it.

So I prayed for the winning lottery ticket.

Man was I excited. I thought I had found a sure way of getting my answer, and I was going to win one way or another. I went down to the convenience store and bought a lottery ticket. The cashier said good luck. I thought, and may have said, I don't need luck. I got home with my lottery ticket, and I prayed over that lottery ticket, giving thanks to God for the millions of dollars He was about to give me.

Finally, the day of the drawing came. Something miraculous did happen. I did not have a single number match on that ticket. I thought, man, this Bible and Jesus stuff is bogus.

But something strange happened. I couldn't help but think about Jesus and all I had learned about His teachings. Something just seemed right about it. Perhaps there was something I was missing.

So I went back to the Bible and continued reading, for some reason I flipped to the book of James. There it was.

James 4:1-10

**What causes fights and quarrels among you? Don't they come
from your desires that battle within you? 2 You desire but do not
have, so you kill. You covet but you cannot get what you want, so
you quarrel and fight. You do not have because you do not ask God.
3 When you ask, you do not receive, because you ask with wrong
motives, that you may spend what you get on your pleasures.**

**4 You adulterous people, don't you know that friendship with
the world means enmity against God? Therefore, anyone who
chooses to be a friend of the world becomes an enemy of God. 5
Or do you think Scripture says without reason that he jealously
longs for the spirit he has caused to dwell in us? 6 But he gives us
more grace. That is why Scripture says:**

"God opposes the proud
but shows favor to the humble."

**7 Submit yourselves, then, to God. Resist the devil, and he will
flee from you. 8 Come near to God and he will come near to you.
Wash your hands, you sinners, and purify your hearts, you
double-minded. 9 Grieve, mourn and wail. Change your laughter
to mourning and your joy to gloom. 10 Humble yourselves before
the Lord, and he will lift you up.**

You want to talk about a ton of conviction falling on a person. I was cut right to the heart. I knew I was found out. There was something I was missing alright. I was missing just about everything.

I remember praying to the Lord and asking Him to forgive me. I also remember asking God to give me wisdom and understanding.

James 1:5

If any of you lacks wisdom, you should ask God, who gives generously to all without finding fault, and it will be given to you.

Here I am praying and asking God for understanding, and my mind became focused on one word, **faith**. I remembered all the times when Jesus was healing people and He mentioned their faith. (Matthew 9:22; Matthew 15:28; Mark 10:52)

At other times, Jesus said He could not heal because people did not have faith.

Mark 8:11-13

**11 The Pharisees came and began to question Jesus. To test him,
they asked him for a sign from heaven. 12 He sighed deeply and
said, "Why does this generation ask for a sign? Truly I tell you,
no sign will be given to it." 13 Then he left them, got back into the
boat and crossed to the other side.**

Jesus does not give a sign from heaven when asked. He called them an evil and perverse generation for seeking signs. Jesus was right in front of them doing all these signs, but none of them were good enough. They always wanted more signs, more evidence, more reasons to believe.

The truth is, for some people, it doesn't matter how much evidence you put in front of them. They have already cast their verdict and are unwilling to examine the evidence.

If you look long enough, you can find someone who will put before you the evidence you are willing to look at. That is, whatever provides the answer you are looking for, whatever supports the side you desire to believe.

In today's world where relativism and pluralism are so widely accepted, there is so much encouragement for people not to believe in an Absolute Truth. People rationalize, justify, minimize, excuse, and flat out deny, all evidence to the contrary.

At that time, I was in a real quandary. Part of me that wanted to believe and part of me wanted to keep living life on my terms. This was one of the first times I remember feeling very strongly that the Lord was speaking to me.

The Lord knew I was wrestling with all this. I had prayed for understanding, and here the Lord was to answer that prayer. I felt the Lord say to me, in my mind and my heart, "Chad, if you want to see my presence in your life, you are going to have to have faith in Me."

I asked the Lord, "What is it about faith that I am not getting?" After all, I did go out and buy that lottery ticket. Isn't that acting on faith?"

I felt the Lord answer me, "Chad, if you have faith in Me, you will stop testing Me and just start doing your best to live with Me in your life.

Trust the Bible is my Word which I have given you to guide you in life. Do your best to follow it and continue to study and learn from Me."

I felt a sense of conviction that a powerful truth had come to me. I had to get off the fence. I had to stop living a double life. I was what the Bible calls "double minded." Part of me was living according to my old ways, and a part of me was living with the Lord.

James 1:6-8

6 But when you ask, you must believe and not doubt, because the
one who doubts is like a wave of the sea, blown and tossed by the
wind. 7 That person should not expect to receive anything from
the Lord. 8 Such a person is double-minded and unstable in all
they do.

I had not come to a verdict in my trial of Jesus, but now I believed that I could not go forward without a firm decision. I knew I could not keep trying to live in two worlds, with two opposing sets of values.

I was scared, nervous and anxious. If I proclaimed that Jesus is Lord, He is the Messiah, and accepted Him as the Savior of my life, then I would have to start living life in a new way.

I wasn't sure what this new life was going to be like, or how it would affect my friendship with others. What I was nervous about was that I knew there were some things I'd have to give up that I didn't want to stop doing. Was I willing to surrender these things to the Lord?

CHAPTER 9

Counting the Cost

I started thinking about some of the things I had read in the Bible and considered what all I would have to give up. I knew that I did not want to be another "hypocritical Christian." If I was going to accept Jesus to be who He and the Bible says He is, then I was going to have to make some significant changes in my life.

Giving up a life of debauchery

Romans 13:13

Let us behave decently, as in the daytime, not in carousing and drunkenness, not in sexual immorality and debauchery, not in dissension and jealousy.

2 Corinthians 12:21

I am afraid that when I come again my God will humble me before you, and I will be grieved over many who have sinned earlier and have not repented of the impurity, sexual sin and debauchery in which they have indulged.

Galatians 5:19

The acts of the flesh are obvious: sexual immorality, impurity and debauchery;

Ephesians 5:18

Do not get drunk on wine, which leads to debauchery. Instead, be filled with the Spirit,

1 Peter 4:3

For you have spent enough time in the past doing what pagans choose to do—living in debauchery, lust, drunkenness, orgies, carousing and detestable idolatry.

We, humans, are strange creatures. The very things I knew I would have to give up were like a bitter-sweet, double-edged, sword. I can't tell you the times I cried out to the Lord asking Him to take these desires away from me. I can't tell you about all the stories that lead to guilt and shame, and even self-hatred. In seeking out this life of debauchery, I had created a prison for myself that I didn't know how to escape from.

Romans 7:15-25

[15] I do not understand what I do. For what I want to do I do not do,
but what I hate I do. [16] And if I do what I do not want to do, I agree
that the law is good.[17] As it is, it is no longer I myself who do it, but
it is sin living in me. [18] For I know that good itself does not dwell
in me, that is, in my sinful nature. For I have the desire to do what
is good, but I cannot carry it out. [19] For I do not do the good I want
to do, but the evil I do not want to do—this I keep on doing.[20] Now
if I do what I do not want to do, it is no longer I who do it, but it is
sin living in me that does it.

21 So I find this law at work: Although I want to do good, evil is
right there with me. 22 For in my inner being I delight in God's
law; 23 but I see another law at work in me, waging war against
the law of my mind and making me a prisoner of the law of sin at
work within me. 24 What a wretched man I am! Who will rescue
me from this body that is subject to death? 25 Thanks be to God,
who delivers me through Jesus Christ our Lord!

That was me to the "T". A man struggling to do the right thing, while inwardly desiring and outwardly acting on the wrong things.

I knew if I continued in my lifestyle, it was only a matter of time before I either died of an overdose or ended up in prison. Of course, death was an option, and somewhere inside I had a death-wish because I thought death would set me free. So I wasn't concerned about dying so much as the pain of living. With my luck, it was more likely that I would end up in jail for doing something stupid while I was high or intoxicated. Sooner or later, the dangerous road I lived was sure to catch up to me in one way or another.

I was a prisoner of my sinful desires. The truth is, sin appeals to our flesh. Like Eve in the Garden of Eden, we look at it long enough and it begins to look pleasing and desirable to us. It's like the person who drinks to get the buzz; that part seems appealing. However, what we don't consider is the hangover, the after-effect it has on us and our lives.

There is a chain reaction of events that gets set off when we choose to sin. This chain reaction is not what we desire, but it's the law of cause and effect. Or, should I say, the law of consequences.

When I got away with things, I was encouraged to continue. I began to get a false sense of confidence. I felt that I knew how to do things in a smarter or better way than others, how not to get caught.

But eventually things catch up, and the consequences affected my life in many ways. I wasn't just hurting myself. The things I was doing (that I thought only affected me) were also affecting those I loved. I brought emotional pain and stress on my family who worried for me.

Here are some common effects of sin that I have experienced and I am sure many other people have too. (This is by no means an exhaustive list but perhaps you can identify with some of it.)

- Loss of job
- Financial ruin
- Poor health - disease
- Loss of home
- Broken relationships
- Jail or other legal issues
- Guilt
- Shame
- Self-hatred
- Physical and emotional pain
- Death

Sin leads to chaos, and chaos by its nature is unmanageable. We try to control it. We try to correct it. We try to take charge of the situation. The sin of pride even allows us to lie to ourselves. We tell ourselves we can somehow manage it, or live at peace with it. But ultimately, sin reveals itself for what it truly is a cruel tool of the devil which reveals the depravity within us.

The Bible says in **Romans 6:23 - For the wages of sin is death, but the gift of God is eternal life in Christ Jesus our Lord.**

Sin eventually leads to a negative outcome. It promises pleasure today, but there is always a hidden cost that shows itself later. The devil, the father of sin, does not want us to consider the long term consequences. He wants to keep us short-term focused.

In contrast, God wants to set us free from sin, to live long-term focused, and receive all the benefits of being His child and life in His Kingdom. The promise we read in Romans 6:23 is that God's gift to us is life (a blessing that is given to us freely), in Jesus Christ. Jesus taught us plainly when He said **(John 10:10), "The thief comes only to steal and kill and destroy; I have come that they may have life, and have it to the full."**

What Jesus was offering me was like the opening of a door to a jail cell. He was allowing me to walk straight out of my prison. The door was in front of me, and it was wide open. There was nothing to prevent me from walking through the open door. The question was, would I?

Why was this so hard? You would think it would have been an easy choice, but somehow I was grieving what I felt I was losing. I didn't want to let go of the very sinful life that had harmed me so deeply.

I would later come to see this like being in an abusive relationship. My girlfriend (my sinful desires) was one mean woman. She was psychotic and dangerous, yet she offered me pleasure. She was attractive, and I loved her in spite of what she did to me. I knew the times of pleasure with her were few, and the chaos of being with her was painful. I knew ultimately things would get ugly, yet I didn't want to break things off with her completely.

Consider the story of Israel traveling between Egypt and the Promised Land.

God had heard the cries of his people in Egypt. Hebrew people were slaves there. They were used and abused. They asked the Lord to deliver them, and so the Lord sent a reluctant servant, named Moses, to lead them out of this land of slavery and pain.

The people of Israel were a bit nervous and hesitant to follow Moses at first. But as they witnessed the miracle of the plagues, and God's protection and blessings they got the courage to leave.

God told them He had a better life for them in a better place. A land flowing with milk and honey, a place where the crops were fruitful, the land was fertile, and it would be theirs.

Jesus, like Moses to Israel, was that good friend encouraging me to leave that old psychotic girl alone and come with Him to find a better life. Why was I so slow to walk away?

I don't have an answer other than to say, I didn't know how good life could really be. I did not know the heights or depths He could take me to. I did not know that He had a wife and kids waiting for me. I didn't know how fulfilling and rewarding life with Him could be. I didn't realize that He had a promised land for me if only I would follow Him.

I continued to struggle with all the false images I had in my head of what it meant to be a Christian. I thought I would have to be like a monk in a monastery and not be allowed to have fun. I had no idea just how much peace and joy I could have.

Every time I started to make the commitment to turn my life over to Jesus, I would start thinking about "Egypt" and what I was leaving behind, just like Israel did.

Exodus 16:3

The Israelites said to them, "If only we had died by the LORD's hand in Egypt! There we sat around pots of meat and ate all the food we wanted, but you have brought us out into this desert to starve this entire assembly to death."

Surely God must get a good laugh at how we attempt to rationalize life. We are like blind people declaring how clearly we see. We somehow convince ourselves that what we see and think is always true.

I started to realize the issue was that I wasn't trusting God. I was reading about God and had started going to church, but I was still uncommitted to Him. When was I going to release control over to Him?

Had I not already shown myself to be untrustworthy? Had I not shown myself that I didn't know how to live life in a way where I could experience a true and lasting peace? And yet I was not willing to trust God!

This is exactly the point in which God was challenging me. It was time for me to lay down all my reasoning, rationalizing, excusing, justifying and everything else that was hindering me. Now more than ever, God was calling, "Who do you say I am? Will you follow me?"

CHAPTER 10

The Verdict – Who is Jesus?

Coming to accept what the Bible had to say about Jesus.

Jesus is the Word – the Word became flesh

John 1:1-2

In the beginning was the Word, and the Word was with God, and the Word was God. [2] He was with God in the beginning.

At first, it was difficult for me to accept that Jesus was God in the flesh. Early in my journey, I thought of Jesus as more of a prophet, someone the Spirit of God rested upon to teach us God's will and to help humanity get back on track. But if He was God's prophet or messenger, I had to consider His message.

He not only taught by giving instructions on how to live but He also taught how to correctly understand the Law given in the Old Testament and God's desire. He also spoke very specifically on Himself and who He was.

John 14:6-11

[6] Jesus answered, "I am the way and the truth and the life. No one comes to the Father except through me. [7] If you really know me,

**you will know my Father as well. From now on, you do know him
and have seen him."**

**8 Philip said, "Lord, show us the Father and that will be enough
for us."**

**9 Jesus answered: "Don't you know me, Philip, even after I have
been among you such a long time? Anyone who has seen me
has seen the Father. How can you say, 'Show us the Father'? 10
Don't you believe that I am in the Father, and that the Father
is in me? The words I say to you I do not speak on my own
authority. Rather, it is the Father, living in me, who is doing his
work. 11 Believe me when I say that I am in the Father and the
Father is in me; or at least believe on the evidence of the works
themselves.**

Up to this point, Jesus was my teacher (rabbi) helping me understand the will of God. I admired Jesus and his heart-filled compassion for sinners, a category I knew without a doubt that I belonged to. I also knew Jesus called me to be His disciple.

Jesus challenged me to be a better man. Then, He challenged me to be a Godly man. My admiration for Jesus began to be transformed into loving Him. My understanding of who Jesus was began to change. By Jesus' words He proclaimed to us all that He, in fact, was the Messiah, the King of the Jews, the Father, the great I AM.

As I looked again at His trial and crucifixion, my heart broke as it finally became clear to me exactly what had occurred. The Creator, God of all the universe, stepped down from His heavenly throne to become one with His creation. He came to reveal Himself fully, knowing He would be rejected. But He was willing to do this, because by doing this, He would become the required sacrifice to cleanse us of our sins.

Hebrews 1:1-3

**In the past God spoke to our ancestors through the prophets at
many times and in various ways, 2 but in these last days he has
spoken to us by his Son, whom he appointed heir of all things,
and through whom also he made the universe. 3 The Son is the
radiance of God's glory and the exact representation of his being,
sustaining all things by his powerful word. After he had provided
purification for sins, he sat down at the right hand of the Majesty
in heaven.**

Hebrews 10:1-10

**The law is only a shadow of the good things that are coming—
not the realities themselves. For this reason it can never, by
the same sacrifices repeated endlessly year after year, make
perfect those who draw near to worship. 2 Otherwise, would they
not have stopped being offered? For the worshipers would have
been cleansed once for all, and would no longer have felt guilty
for their sins. 3 But those sacrifices are an annual reminder of
sins. 4 It is impossible for the blood of bulls and goats to take
away sins.**

5 Therefore, when Christ came into the world, he said:

**"Sacrifice and offering you did not desire,
  but a body you prepared for me;
6 with burnt offerings and sin offerings
  you were not pleased.
7 Then I said, 'Here I am—it is written about me in the scroll—
  I have come to do your will, my God.'**

**8 First he said, "Sacrifices and offerings, burnt offerings and sin
offerings you did not desire, nor were you pleased with them"—
though they were offered in accordance with the law. 9 Then he
said, "Here I am, I have come to do your will." He sets aside the**

first to establish the second.[10] And by that will, we have been made holy through the sacrifice of the body of Jesus Christ once for all.

What it is saying here is that when God gave the Law to Moses and Israel and the ritual practices of animal sacrifices, the animals were symbolically accepting the guilt of the sinner whom the sacrifice was offered for. However, the person's sacrifice did not cover all sins for all times. It was only a symbolic action that needed to be repeated because we are sinners who continue to sin.

Christ, the Son of God, God in the flesh, giving Himself up as a sacrifice was the last sacrifice needed. This is the blessing of the Last Supper, the mystery of communion, the greatest gift ever given for the good of humanity.

Jesus is the Passover Lamb

Mark 14:12

[12] On the first day of the Festival of Unleavened Bread, when it was customary to sacrifice the Passover lamb, Jesus' disciples asked him, "Where do you want us to go and make preparations for you to eat the Passover?"

The Festival of Unleavened Bread began as a tradition for Israel to remember what the Lord had done for them by setting them free from slavery in Egypt. It was a time of embracing their history as they recalled how God's favor had released them from bondage to Egypt.

This is the same story of Moses I mentioned earlier in the book. Moses had gone to Pharaoh demanding that he let God's people go. Pharaoh refused, and God then sent ten plagues, each with a call for Pharaoh to repent. Each one also revealed to Israel how God was acting on their behalf.

You can read the story in its entirety in Exodus. However, I want to focus on the tenth and final plague found in Exodus, chapter 12. The tenth plague required Israel to select a perfect male lamb or goat, roast it whole and then eat all of the lamb. The blood of the lamb was to be smeared on the doorpost of the house in which the meal had been eaten. When the Angel of the Lord came through Egypt that night and killed the firstborn male in every household that did not have the blood on the doorpost. After this Pharaoh finally gave in and allowed the Israelites to leave Egypt.

Only those who had participated in eating the Passover Lamb were saved. Only those who were sealed with the sign of the blood smeared on the doorposts were saved. And it was during the Last Supper (which took place on the very night that the Passover meal was to be eaten in remembrance) that Jesus proclaimed to His disciples that He was the Passover Lamb.

He was fulfilling the will of God. By eating the bread (a symbol of His body), and by drinking the wine (a symbol of His blood), we are to be saved from the judgment to come. That is, we are to accept the offering Jesus gave in Himself for the forgiveness of our sins.

Just as in the Passover meal and the tenth plague God gave a warning, He also set the terms of what would happen and how people could be saved. God is the only one who gets to decide these matters. It was not up for a vote then, nor did it go to the polls of public opinion. God set the terms and still does. The question is, will we take Him at His word and will we bring ourselves into agreement with His desires for us?

So, if Jesus is the Passover Lamb, what does this mean?

Propitiation – Jesus is my Savior

Romans 3:21-26

**21 But now the righteousness of God apart from the law is
revealed, being witnessed by the Law and the Prophets, 22 even
the righteousness of God, through faith in Jesus Christ, to all
and on all who believe. For there is no difference; 23 for all have
sinned and fall short of the glory of God, 24 being justified freely
by His grace through the redemption that is in Christ Jesus, 25
whom God set forth as a propitiation by His blood, through faith,
to demonstrate His righteousness, because in His forbearance
God had passed over the sins that were previously committed,
26 to demonstrate at the present time His righteousness, that He
might be just and the justifier of the one who has faith in Jesus.**

Dr. Robert McGee author of *Search for Significance*, defines propitiation this way: "The wrath of someone who has been unjustly wronged, has been satisfied.[1]"

In other Bible translations, the word propitiation is interpreted as "atoning sacrifice", meaning to bring us back to being at one with God through the sacrifice made in Jesus Christ.

Remember, all sin derives from us choosing to take God off the throne of our lives where He should rightly be. In essence, we unwittingly stage a coup and kick the Lord out. We take over and often place other things, people or philosophies in the place where God should be.

Thus, all sin is against God. The Bible helps us to understand this in the book of Romans:

[1] McGee, Robert S. *The Search for Significance*. Nashville: W Publishing Group. 2003, pg 88.

Romans 1:18 - [18] The wrath of God is being revealed from heaven against all the godlessness and wickedness of people, who suppress the truth by their wickedness,

Romans 1:21 - [21] For although they knew God, they neither glorified him as God nor gave thanks to him, but their thinking became futile and their foolish hearts were darkened.

Romans 1:28 - [28] Furthermore, just as they did not think it worthwhile to retain the knowledge of God, so God gave them over to a depraved mind, so that they do what ought not to be done.

Romans 2:1 - You, therefore, have no excuse, you who pass judgment on someone else, for at whatever point you judge another, you are condemning yourself, because you who pass judgment do the same things.

Romans 3:23 - [23] for all have sinned and fall short of the glory of God,

Through our sins, we are all worthy of God's wrath. We have abandoned God's desires for us and His laws.

Jesus reminds us what the two greatest commandments are in Matthew 22:34-40:

[34] Hearing that Jesus had silenced the Sadducees, the Pharisees got together.[35] One of them, an expert in the law, tested him with this question: [36] "Teacher, which is the greatest commandment in the Law?"

[37] Jesus replied: "'Love the Lord your God with all your heart and with all your soul and with all your mind.' [38] This is the first and greatest commandment.[39] And the second is like it: 'Love your

neighbor as yourself.' [40] All the Law and the Prophets hang on these two commandments."

We have all broken the two greatest commandments at some point in our lives. We have not ALWAYS loved the Lord with ALL our heart, mind, soul, and strength. Nor have we ALWAYS loved our neighbor as ourselves. If you have kept all the other commandments but failed in either, or both, of these areas you have still sinned against God.

Why must there be a price paid for our sins? Why must God's wrath be fulfilled? Isn't He a kind, loving God?

Yes, God is kind and loving, but He is also just. The issue is that sin, or rebellious behavior, left unchecked will usher in chaos and pain even for innocent bystanders. You cannot have both chaos and order. You cannot have sin without consequences.

Let's start looking at it by considering what type of community we would love to live in for all eternity. Of course, as a Christian, I am referring to Heaven.

In Heaven,

- Will people be allowed to continue to sin in heaven? If so, then we will have the same world in heaven that we have here and now. Is that really what we desire? Is that the better life to come? NO!!!!
- Will there be stealing, rape, murder, covetousness, adultery, lies, sickness, death, selfishness or any other sinful behavior in Heaven? No. Why, because God will not allow it and that is for our benefit.

God has made a judgment against such things, and we cannot live in God's Kingdom and under our own set of rules. God has allowed us to experience the folly of our ways in this world so that when we go to

Heaven we will have a greater understanding of why we need to be faithful to God and all His ways.

God's ultimate desire is that we live in peace and harmony with Him and with one another. To live in sin is not to be in harmony with God's desires for us.

When I take a good look at this world it is easy to see the dysfunctional ways of this world are all a result of sin. God allows us the opportunity to make our own choice about whether we will follow His will for us, or not. God assures us that He will only put up with this behavior for so long before He intervenes. He intervenes because He loves us and when He does intervene His judgments will be just and fair.

God has provided an opportunity for us to escape the judgment to come. He did so by coming to earth and performing miracles so that we might believe in Him. He raised Himself from the dead and ascended into Heaven in full view of many witnesses. In doing this, He fulfilled many scriptural promises that were written hundreds of years before He even came to earth.

Through believing in Him and giving our lives back to His authority, that we begin to find the new life He offers us. This is where becoming "born again" comes into the scene.

CHAPTER 11

Born Again – Getting a New Beginning

2 Corinthians 5:17

Therefore, if anyone is in Christ, the new creation has come: The old has gone, the new is here!

As I came to accept what the Bible was teaching me about Jesus, myself, and God's desires for me, I realized that I was at odds with my new beliefs. How I was living was inconsistent with what God wanted of me. Was I going to truly make a commitment to live as the Lord would have me live or was I going to continue to live life on my terms?

Jesus taught on one occasion saying:

Mark 2:22

[22] And no one pours new wine into old wineskins. Otherwise, the wine will burst the skins, and both the wine and the wineskins will be ruined. No, they pour new wine into new wineskins."

That is exactly what I was doing at the time. I was trying to be filled with the new wine (Jesus in me), yet I was still the old unchanged wine skin (living on my terms). What needed to happen? How was I going to change? Was I going to change?

That's when Jesus helped me to understand what being born again really meant. We read here in John chapter 3.

**Now there was a Pharisee, a man named Nicodemus who was a
member of the Jewish ruling council. 2 He came to Jesus at night
and said, "Rabbi, we know that you are a teacher who has come
from God. For no one could perform the signs you are doing if God
were not with him."**

**3 Jesus replied, "Very truly I tell you, no one can see the kingdom
of God unless they are born again."**

**4 "How can someone be born when they are old?" Nicodemus
asked. "Surely they cannot enter a second time into their mother's
womb to be born!"**

**5 Jesus answered, "Very truly I tell you, no one can enter the
kingdom of God unless they are born of water and the Spirit. 6
Flesh gives birth to flesh, but the Spirit gives birth to spirit. 7 You
should not be surprised at my saying, 'You must be born again.' 8
The wind blows wherever it pleases. You hear its sound, but you
cannot tell where it comes from or where it is going. So it is with
everyone born of the Spirit."**

9 "How can this be?" Nicodemus asked.

**10 "You are Israel's teacher," said Jesus, "and do you not understand
these things? 11 Very truly I tell you, we speak of what we know,
and we testify to what we have seen, but still you people do not
accept our testimony. 12 I have spoken to you of earthly things
and you do not believe; how then will you believe if I speak of
heavenly things? 13 No one has ever gone into heaven except the
one who came from heaven—the Son of Man. 14 Just as Moses
lifted up the snake in the wilderness, so the Son of Man must
be lifted up, 15 that everyone who believes may have eternal life
in him."**

**16 For God so loved the world that he gave his one and only Son,
that whoever believes in him shall not perish but have eternal
life. 17 For God did not send his Son into the world to condemn
the world, but to save the world through him. 18 Whoever believes
in him is not condemned, but whoever does not believe stands
condemned already because they have not believed in the name
of God's one and only Son. 19 This is the verdict: Light has come
into the world, but people loved darkness instead of light because
their deeds were evil. 20 Everyone who does evil hates the light,
and will not come into the light for fear that their deeds will be
exposed. 21 But whoever lives by the truth comes into the light,
so that it may be seen plainly that what they have done has been
done in the sight of God.**

In my understanding, the first birth is us being born in the flesh. We grew up learning to live according to the desires of our flesh. We did what our flesh wanted us to do. Being born-again, the second birth, is a spiritual birth that we have at some point during our lives. It is changing our commitment from living for the desires of the flesh to learning to live to fulfill the desires of God.

God's Holy Spirit comes to us who make this commitment to be a helper to empower us to make these changes.

John 14:15-17

**15 "If you love me, keep my commands. 16 And I will ask the Father,
and he will give you another advocate to help you and be with you
forever— 17 the Spirit of truth.**

The advocate Jesus is referring to is the Holy Spirit. The Holy Spirit is to help us, not to do everything for us. We have to choose to work in cooperation with the Spirit of God, through following His Word, the Holy Bible. If we truly desire to live by the Spirit, then we must learn to exercise the authority God has given us to have mastery over our flesh.

EVERYONE is born in the flesh. Not everyone has been born of the Spirit. Are you willing to surrender your flesh over to the Spirit of God?

Getting back to where I was at this point in my journey, I was living in a little apartment in Buffalo, Texas, above a store where I was working for my dad. I was having the spiritual wrestling match of my life. God was speaking to my heart asking me to go all in for Him. I knew there was still a disconnect between my changing beliefs and how I was living.

As I was trying to understand what it was God was wanting of me, I came across some other passages of scripture that challenged me.

Matthew 16:25

For whoever wants to save their life will lose it, but whoever loses their life for me will find it.

Galatians 2:20

I have been crucified with Christ and I no longer live, but Christ lives in me. The life I now live in the body, I live by faith in the Son of God, who loved me and gave himself for me.

Ephesians 4:17

So I tell you this, and insist on it in the Lord, that you must no longer live as the Gentiles do, in the futility of their thinking.

What these passages said to me is that I needed to stop living for myself and start living for the Lord. I needed to stop rationalizing and protecting my old way of life. If I was ever going to find the real truth in scripture and experience the real freedom that Christ offers, I needed to let the old me die and start all over again with Jesus showing me the way.

Romans 6:5-14

**5 For if we have been united with him in a death like his, we will
certainly also be united with him in a resurrection like his. 6 For
we know that our old self was crucified with him so that the body
ruled by sin might be done away with, that we should no longer
be slaves to sin— 7 because anyone who has died has been set
free from sin.**

**8 Now if we died with Christ, we believe that we will also live with
him. 9 For we know that since Christ was raised from the dead, he
cannot die again; death no longer has mastery over him. 10 The
death he died, he died to sin once for all; but the life he lives, he
lives to God.**

**11 In the same way, count yourselves dead to sin but alive to God
in Christ Jesus. 12 Therefore do not let sin reign in your mortal
body so that you obey its evil desires. 13 Do not offer any part of
yourself to sin as an instrument of wickedness, but rather offer
yourselves to God as those who have been brought from death to
life; and offer every part of yourself to him as an instrument of
righteousness. 14 For sin shall no longer be your master, because
you are not under the law, but under grace.**

And there it was. Was I willing to consider myself and the life I had left dead? Was I willing to give up ownership of myself and willing to truly live for Christ?

I can't remember the number of times I should have physically died. I knew many people who lived the same type of life I had that did die. Why had the Lord allowed me to live? I concluded He must have some purpose for me.

God challenged me to stop testing Him and start trusting Him. At that moment, I finally surrendered. I got down on my knees, bowed my head before God, and asked God to forgive me for all of my sins. I professed Jesus was the Son of God, and I would follow Him. I would stop living life on my terms, and I committed to living life the way the Bible was teaching me, to the best of my imperfect ability.

I felt God's joy wash over me. That is the only way I know how to explain it. I felt like a ton of weight had been lifted off me, that shackles had fallen off, and I was free to walk out of the prison I had lived in for so long. Jesus had opened the door long ago, but now I was choosing to walk through it, and follow Him. I was born-again.

For 30 years I had lived life on my terms, based on my understanding. I had taught myself how to obey my flesh and fulfill my sinful desires. Now it was time for me to learn to live life on His terms and lean on His understanding. No holding back.

Proverbs 3:5-6

5 Trust in the LORD with all your heart and lean not on your own understanding; 6 in all your ways submit to him, and he will make your paths straight.

Time to Start Pruning the Branches – Getting Rid of the Old and Putting on the New

I knew I had to make some changes and I sensed that adventurous times were ahead. I expected there would be some difficulties but I knew surrendering to the Lord was what I needed to do. So I prayed for God to help me be strong and have courage.

Joshua 1:7-9

"Be strong and very courageous. Be careful to obey all the law my servant Moses gave you; do not turn from it to the right or to the left, that you may be successful wherever you go. 8 Keep this Book of the Law always on your lips; meditate on it day

and night, so that you may be careful to do everything written in it. Then you will be prosperous and successful. [9] Have I not commanded you? Be strong and courageous. Do not be afraid; do not be discouraged, for the LORD your God will be with you wherever you go."

This passage from Joshua has always been special to me. Joshua received these words from the Lord just after Moses died. He was about to step into the leadership role for Israel, which was the role the Lord had prepared him for. He was being charged by God to be faithful.

I identified with Joshua, because like him, I was heading into a new land, a Promised Land, and I did not know or understand all that I would have to face.

I also believe that just as God spoke these words to Joshua, He speaks to us today. God desires us to be faithful to His Word. He calls us to be a disciplined and faithful people. He calls for our loyalty. He asks us to be conscientious of what we are doing and how we are representing Him on this earth.

He tells us that we need to be strong and courageous for a reason. Life is not going to be easy. In fact, there are going to be battles ahead. Some of our battles might even be with people we love. We are going to have to face the enemy (the enemy is not other people, it is lies people believe) and take a hold of what God promises us.

It's not an easy life we are called to when we choose to follow Jesus. I have become convinced that we cannot be weak minded and be a faithful Christian at the same time. However, if we can be strong and faithful, it's worth fighting the battles that lie ahead. The journey is well worth it.

Jesus helps us understand how to give our lives over to God in His teaching about the vine and the branches.

John 15 - The Vine and the Branches

15 "I am the true vine, and my Father is the gardener. 2 He cuts off every branch in me that bears no fruit, while every branch that does bear fruit he prunes so that it will be even more fruitful. 3 You are already clean because of the word I have spoken to you. 4 Remain in me, as I also remain in you. No branch can bear fruit by itself; it must remain in the vine. Neither can you bear fruit unless you remain in me.

5 "I am the vine; you are the branches. If you remain in me and I in you, you will bear much fruit; apart from me you can do nothing. 6 If you do not remain in me, you are like a branch that is thrown away and withers; such branches are picked up, thrown into the fire and burned. 7 If you remain in me and my words remain in you, ask whatever you wish, and it will be done for you. 8 This is to my Father's glory, that you bear much fruit, showing yourselves to be my disciples.

Even up until the day before I surrendered my life to Christ, I was still drinking fairly regularly and smoking pot occasionally. Although my aggressive chasing after women had slowed down greatly as I was getting to know Jesus, I still had the wrong view of women. All of these things needed to change.

More than just needing to stop doing the things that were sinful in God's eyes, I needed to discover what my purpose was. I needed to find out what God wanted me to do with my life.

During this time of committing myself to the Lord, I learned a lot about myself. I was amazed to see how truly weak I was and how easily I could be tempted to leave God and sin. It seemed like temptation was everywhere in those early days. I knew I could not sit around and be idle because when I got bored it was a trigger for me to return to my old lifestyle. I learned I had many other triggers as well. When I felt stressed, I would be tempted to have a beer or smoke a joint. If I saw an attractive girl who was dressed immodestly, I would feel the temptation to return to sexual immorality.

Another trigger was when I talked to old friends who were still living according to my old lifestyle. They would invite me to join them; they didn't mean anything bad by doing so. It was just part of our friendship. But I knew for me it was a temptation and I needed to start putting some space between myself and my old friends and that was hard.

I cared for my friends; I had come to love them and I felt they loved and cared for me. However, I was committing myself to God, so I knew I should not put myself in places where I would be tempted. I wasn't judging them but I wanted to be faithful to God, and I did not trust myself to be with them. I did not trust myself to say no to drinking, drugs, or not engage in other behavior the Lord might find objectionable when I was with them. God was asking me to make some sacrifices for Him.

Romans 12:1-2

Therefore, I urge you, brothers and sisters, in view of God's mercy, to offer your bodies as a living sacrifice, holy and pleasing to God—this is your true and proper worship. [2] Do not conform to the pattern of this world, but be transformed by the renewing of your mind. Then you will be able to test and approve what God's will is—his good, pleasing and perfect will.

It is hard to say, "I need to make sacrifices," and it is even harder to do. Whether we want to admit it or not, we cannot be a Christian without making some sacrifices.

Luckily our sacrifices today do not have to be like those in the Old Testament, and we do not need to kill animals sacrificially. The sacrifice of the animals was God trying to teach us a lesson. Every sin has a consequence; it brings death. The consequences can't be taken back. The amazing part of God's love was being revealed in a subtle way. That is, instead of us shedding our blood for our sinfulness, He allowed for a substitute because even in our sinfulness the Good Father was looking for ways to protect His children. God graciously allowed the animal to pay the price for our sins.

This was also God revealing what He was going to do in Jesus Christ. Jesus became our sacrificial lamb. A Holy and Perfect man paid the price of sinfulness for all humankind. In Jesus, God came to earth and offered Himself as the atoning sacrifice for all of us. That is why we are no longer asked to sacrifice animals as offerings to God. The only sacrifice God asks us to make is to sacrifice the desires of our flesh and live for Him.

Consider this; God is asking us to sacrifice the very things that are harmful to us, that cause us mental, emotional, physical, financial and spiritual pain. God is asking us to sacrifice the behaviors and thoughts that are tearing our world apart. God is giving us a chance to experience this world He created for us, the way it was meant to be experienced. Not at all what it has become today.

Today, the call for me to sacrifice not only means living without sins I used to pursue, but it also means sacrificing to help someone or some cause that God calls me to support. The cutting away of the old dead branches from the vine was learning to leave behind the old life. The pruning, so that I could produce fruit for the Kingdom, was clinging to God and doing His will.

The great thing about God's plan is that in the long run, it benefits everyone. I benefit from the peace and joy that have become a regular part of my life since coming to Christ. My faithfulness to God allows me to do things that benefit others and help make the world a better place. That's the whole fruit metaphor.

If I am doing the work God calls me to do, I am producing "fruit" which is also beneficial to others. The point I'm trying to get across here is that the things God asks us to give up in life are nothing compared to the good we can bring when we truly follow Him. Every sacrifice God asks us to make is a blessing in disguise. Or should I say a blessing coming forth to be received by someone.

Over the years God has taught me that the more I live to do His good will here on earth, the more I am helping to build up His Heavenly Kingdom. I'll talk more about this as I continue sharing my testimony with you.

At this time in my life, God needed me to learn more about His will before He could send me off into the world. Every night when I got home from work, my routine was to cook dinner, give thanks, eat, then I would read the Bible for most of the night just trying to learn more. As I read, God challenged me to cut off more dead branches. Remember, a dead branch is any sinful behavior that does not produce what God desires in our lives.

So I would read something like this:

Matthew 5:27-30

27 "You have heard that it was said, 'You shall not commit adultery."
28 But I tell you that anyone who looks at a woman lustfully has
already committed adultery with her in his heart. 29 If your right
eye causes you to stumble, gouge it out and throw it away. It is
better for you to lose one part of your body than for your whole
body to be thrown into hell. 30 And if your right hand causes you
to stumble, cut it off and throw it away. It is better for you to lose
one part of your body than for your whole body to go into hell.

This passage does not literally advocate cutting off your hand or gouging out your eyes. This is what one author, Jay Adams, calls radical amputation[1]. The intent is the same as that in the message of the

[1] Adams, Jay E. *A Theology of Christian Counseling: More Than Redemption.* Grand Rapids, MI. 1979, pgs 263-266.

vine and the branches: to cut yourself off from the things that will ultimately harm you and others.

The main lesson these verses taught me was that my view of women and my relationships with them was inappropriate. I was treating women like objects only good for satisfying my personal, fleshly desires. The Lord helped me to see that entertaining such thoughts in my head was no different that acting on them. The Lord was asking me to change on the inside, not just on the outside.

So I had to stop participating in all forms of pornography. Whether it was something material like magazines or mental like fantasies where I played director to fulfill my lustful desires. God was using His Word to cut a dead branch out of my life. Whenever God cuts off a dead branch; a destructive, sinful, self-serving area out of your life, God also takes the time to prune other areas for growth that is healthy.

While God was challenging me to cut off old behaviors, He also started to teach me how to respect women and treat them honorably as children of God. The Lord had to teach me this before He could later give Rene and me to one another. When God asks you to give something up, He already has plans for something better, something more rewarding, to give you in its place.

I had to quit using drugs and alcohol so God could one day use me to help others learn how to surrender their lives to the Lord to overcome these devastating addictions. God knows how to take our painful life experiences and turn them into triumphant stories.

I want to let those of you reading this in the early stages of turning your life over to Christ know the journey is well worth it.

CHAPTER 12

Worshipping God – Breaking the Altar of Money

It's interesting what people try to bring with them into their new life in Christ. Or maybe, it's more of what they are too scared to let go of to come fully into their new lives.

Probably most people have seen on TV or heard a story of a heavy set man who gets his hand stuck reaching into a vending machine. The emergency personnel arrives and ask why he is still holding onto the item in the machine. The EMT tells the man to let go of the item and pull his hand out. And of course, the man does so, getting unstuck was as easy as letting go.

It's comical, but unfortunately it's true. I can't tell you how many people I see screaming for help who would be so much better off if they would just let go of a certain behavior or belief.

One area I have noticed many Christians bring into their new life with Christ is their old beliefs about money. People hold on in this area for dear life, not willing to let go and be released to find new freedom.

I have read the writings of some Godly financial stewards, such as Scott Rodin and Brian Kluth. They tell the story of God's upside-down economy. The way to be faithful to God's Kingdom with money is to learn to be open-handed, willing to use it, wherever God leads you.

As we learn to give money where He desires us to give, God sees our faithfulness and blesses us so that we can give even more.

We read in **Malachi 3:6-12**

**6 "I the LORD do not change. So you, the descendants of Jacob, are
not destroyed. 7 Ever since the time of your ancestors you have
turned away from my decrees and have not kept them. Return to
me, and I will return to you," says the LORD Almighty.**

"But you ask, 'How are we to return?'

8 "Will a mere mortal rob God? Yet you rob me.

"But you ask, 'How are we robbing you?'

**"In tithes and offerings. 9 You are under a curse—your whole
nation—because you are robbing me. 10 Bring the whole tithe
into the storehouse, that there may be food in my house. Test me
in this," says the LORD Almighty, "and see if I will not throw open
the floodgates of heaven and pour out so much blessing that there
will not be room enough to store it. 11 I will prevent pests from
devouring your crops, and the vines in your fields will not drop
their fruit before it is ripe," says the LORD Almighty. 12 "Then all
the nations will call you blessed, for yours will be a delightful
land," says the LORD Almighty.**

I started reading more about the tithing and found out that tithe means 10% of one's income. The first fruit. In our modern language, that is gross income, before taxes.

This is where some people will start arguing. The bottom line is this, if you are looking for excuses, justifications, and rationalizations as to why you should not give the full tithe, then finances are an idol in your life. Sorry for not sugar-coating it. Let go of your beliefs about money for a moment and see where God desires to take you.

Here's what I'm talking about. If I am withholding something from God to help myself feel more secure or more in control, then I am robbing God. Not only am I robbing God but I am also unwittingly robbing myself. I am robbing God of trusting Him above all else which robs my relationship with God. I'm robbing myself of the opportunity to experience God as Jehovah Jireh, my Provider.

When you start feeling challenged by the Word of God, you need to be willing to let it challenge you. Let the Word of God disrupt your life. God wants us to grow, but we can't grow and also stay the same. Some people start looking for ways to go back to their comfort zones when they become uncomfortable with the changes God is calling them to make. These are those that the Bible says:

2 Timothy 4:3

3 For the time will come when people will not put up with sound doctrine. Instead, to suit their own desires, they will gather around them a great number of teachers to say what their itching ears want to hear.

You cannot say you trust the Lord and truly want to follow Him, but only when His Word says something you agree with or want it to say. Sometimes the Bible says things that are inconvenient for me in how I want to live my life. The question is, am I going to let God be God? Or am I going to take back the reigns whenever God challenges me in a way that is inconvenient or not how I would like to live?

Matthew 6:24

24 "No one can serve two masters. Either you will hate the one and love the other, or you will be devoted to the one and despise the other. You cannot serve both God and money.

At this time in my life, I felt the Lord asking me if I wanted Him to be Lord of all or only Lord of some?

Did I want His blessings to be over my finances? Then I needed to give my finances to Him on His terms. It's true of finances, and every other area of my life. If I want all of God's blessings on every part of my life, I need to give every part of my life to Him.

Whenever God asks me to give financially to another person or ministry, there is always a blessing that comes back to me. I don't give to get (that is what is wrong with prosperity gospels, they ask the person to give to fulfill selfish desires). The truth is, there are spiritual laws at work. When I give faithfully, I benefit because I am exercising freedom from greed; but more importantly, I grow in being the generous person God desires me to be.

Ultimately God blesses those who are faithful with more because of their faithfulness. I have seen this time and time again in my life.

For me, this part of the journey began with tithing. Tithing is such a hard concept for many people. If you want to see people get riled up quickly, start talking to them about giving the full tithe to the church. The sweetest people can quickly change their demeanor. Why? It's because people have an ownership mentality. I did not come to the full understanding of this principal until much later. I now understand that either everything belongs to God, or nothing belongs to God. You can't have it both ways.

Psalm 24:1

The earth is the LORD's, and everything in it, the world, and all who live in it;

What started in my life as a willingness to sacrifice has grown and developed into a testimony of the ways I have witnessed and experienced God's faithfulness in my life.

My experience with tithing started soon after I surrendered my life to Christ. I wasn't making much money then. I got paid $200 a week. As I read the passage from Malachi 3, I realized this was an area I had not yet given to the Lord.

I was living paycheck to paycheck, didn't have a car and walked to the grocery store to get what I needed (except for the times when my dad could give me a ride). On the road between where I was living and the grocery store was a place called the Lord's Pantry. On several occasions I thought that perhaps I would go in there to see if I qualified for free food. I probably didn't because of pride more than anything else.

I was not in a good financial position, and yet this was when God asked me to start tithing. "Really God?" I thought. Isn't there some sort of exemption for people like me? Shouldn't I have to make enough money to live above the poverty line before I start giving the tithe?

Then I remembered reading the following two passages.

Mark 12:41-44

41 Jesus sat down opposite the place where the offerings were
put and watched the crowd putting their money into the temple
treasury. Many rich people threw in large amounts. 42 But a poor
widow came and put in two very small copper coins, worth only
a few cents.

43 Calling his disciples to him, Jesus said, "Truly I tell you, this
poor widow has put more into the treasury than all the others. 44
They all gave out of their wealth; but she, out of her poverty, put
in everything—all she had to live on."

2 Corinthians 9:7

Each of you should give what you have decided in your heart to give, not reluctantly or under compulsion, for God loves a cheerful giver.

A couple of things I see in these scriptures.

First, Jesus was watching as people put their gifts in the Temple treasury. He is watching still today. He did not speak up against this but was watching people's faithfulness. That is what excited Him so much when He saw the poor widow throw in her two copper coins. It wasn't the amount she gave; it was the percentage she gave – she gave all she had.

From the scripture in Corinthians, I realized that God is willing to meet people where they are at and allow them the opportunity to grow in their giving. We don't need to have our lives together before we start living faithfully to God. What is important to God is that we learn to become cheerful givers. God wants us to learn the spiritual discipline of giving and participate in the blessing of being generous people. When we start living faithfully for God, He puts our lives back together His way.

These scriptures also helped me to see God does not set a limit on giving by asking for the tithe (10%). God gets super excited when we grow to give more than 10%. It's not because He needs the money, it's not about giving to a church budget, it's all about the work God is doing in your heart.

God is trying to help us work on who we are, our character and our nature. A generous heart is what God is focused on developing in us. The act of giving financially means we are free from the bondage of money as our source of security. We are trusting in God and willing to give to help others.

Remember God is trying to help us to be more like Him. God gives to us all the time. He is a generous giver, and it is not just about money. He generously gave us Jesus, His most valued and beloved Son, all for our benefit. That's how much He loves us.

Back to my experiences with God through tithing.

As I was saying, I was making $200 a week. So I started giving $20 a week in the offering plate at church. And I felt good about it. I knew my $20 wasn't making or breaking the church. For me, tithing was all about trusting God and taking Him at His Word. It was about my willingness to grow by being faithful.

One day, as I was walking to the grocery store to pick up some things the Lord's Pantry caught my attention. I felt the Lord urging me to give to the Lord's Pantry. At the grocery store, I picked up a few extra items. On my way home I stopped by the Lord's Pantry and gave them a bag of food. My circumstances had not changed, but I was learning to be a giver.

The Lord was teaching me to live within my means and give from whatever I had. He was also teaching me one of the greatest lessons, the joy of being content with what I had.

CHAPTER 13

Learning to Put the Lord First

Matthew 6:33 - But seek first his kingdom and his righteousness, and all these things will be given to you as well.

Consider this scripture

Matthew 19:16-22

16 Just then a man came up to Jesus and asked, "Teacher, what good thing must I do to get eternal life?"

17 "Why do you ask me about what is good?" Jesus replied. "There is only One who is good. If you want to enter life, keep the commandments."

18 "Which ones?" he inquired.

Jesus replied, "'You shall not murder, you shall not commit adultery,
you shall not steal, you shall not give false testimony, 19 honor your
father and mother,' and 'love your neighbor as yourself.'"

20 "All these I have kept," the young man said. "What do I still lack?"

21 Jesus answered, "If you want to be perfect, go, sell your possessions and give to the poor, and you will have treasure in heaven. Then come, follow me."

22 When the young man heard this, he went away sad, because he had great wealth.

The rich young man had many things and a lot of wealth, but he did not have contentment. He knew there was something he was lacking. That's why he went to Jesus and started asking the questions in the first place. He wasn't there to test Jesus; rather he was looking for something. He knew he had great wealth. He knew what he owned. Yet, he also knew he was incomplete.

When Jesus tells him to keep the commandments, the young man reveals his heart as he asks, "Which ones?"

"Which ones" is asking, what's the bare minimum I need to do? That is the mindset we need to get out of. We need to get into what pastor and author, Mark Batterson, would say is an "ALL IN" mindset. (If you haven't read Mark's book All In, I highly recommend it.)

Jesus challenges this rich young man to go all in. To sell everything he has, give it to the poor, and follow Him. He challenges him to stop withholding from God.

The rich young ruler was only looking at what he was being asked to give up. Unfortunately, he failed to see that what he would gain was far more than what he had. If only he had been willing to trust Jesus and do as the Lord asked.

Galatians 6:7

7 Do not be deceived: God cannot be mocked. A man reaps what he sows.

Consider this.

Moses was given instructions to throw down his staff and it would turn into a snake as a sign that God truly sent him. Moses had to act in obedience trusting God BEFORE the staff would change into a serpent.

Consider Joshua and the battle of Jericho (Joshua 6). He and the army of Israel had to march around the city of Jericho one time for six days, and then on the seventh day march around it seven times. The walls did not come crashing down until they had completed everything the Lord asked them to do.

I can't find anywhere in the Bible where God rewards people for doing only a portion of what He asked. However; I do find throughout scripture people who veer from God's plan in some way bring trouble upon themselves. When people do all that God asks, He rewards them generously.

Think about the miracle of the wine for the wedding at Cana (John 2). Mary knew what to do. She told the servants to do EVERYTHING Jesus asked them to do. They were given the arduous task of filling up six large stone jars of water that held about 20 to 30 gallons each.

That might not sound like a big deal until you put it into context. They did not have plumbing the way we know it. They didn't just run a water hose to fill the jars. They had to go to the well (probably a walk of a half mile away, one way), draw water from the well and then carry filled containers by hand, back to the stone jars to fill them up.

Six stone jars, 20 to 30 gallons each. That is somewhere between 120 to 180 gallons of water they carried. If you have ever picked up a 5-gallon bucket full of water, you might understand what a large task this was. They were working awfully hard, faithfully and obediently carrying water, although they needed wine.

They had no idea how this was going to work. They had never witnessed Jesus doing anything like this before. Perhaps they were murmuring to themselves the entire time they were carrying that water, thinking, "I don't see how this is going to help."

I prefer to think that perhaps those servants were carrying that water with some joy and excitement, thinking to themselves, "I can't wait to see what Jesus does with this!"

They had to fill all six jars to the brim.

If they would have stopped short, they would not have witnessed the miracle and received the victory. Too often, we give ourselves permission to stop short of being faithful to God. We miss our chance at seeing a miracle. It couldn't be "close enough." The jars had to be all the way full.

That's the question the rich young man was asking Jesus. How much is close enough? Which commandments do I really need to follow because I don't feel like doing them all? What's just enough to skate by?

Too many people are skating by. What a shame! I say that with sadness in my heart because these people are missing the opportunity to see what God has in store for them. Just like the rich young man, he could have been one of the twelve disciples. He could have been one of the ones who was sent out to preach the gospel and cast out demons in Jesus' name.

Think about the experiences he missed out on because he had his priorities backward. We shouldn't put God on the backburner because of what we see as wise in our own eyes. I'm sure the rich young man felt he was better off by being smart in a worldly way. That is a temptation we all face.

The truth, the lesson for this young man and for all of us is hidden in plain sight. Right there in the story he asks, "What good thing must I do to inherit eternal life?" I'm sure he asked with confidence because with his wealth he could accomplish an awful lot.

Jesus first reminds him WHO is good. Only God.

Why is this important?

How do you judge how good you are? By the things you do, correct?

Jesus is gently reminding this young man he should be resting in who God is, not in his own works. But Jesus, so as not to embarrass the young man openly reminds him of the commandments. What is key here is what Jesus did not include!

Jesus went to the final six commandments with a little bit of a twist. Jesus rephrased, I believe intentionally, the tenth commandment. The tenth commandment in Exodus 20:17 – Do not covet your neighbor's house or anything he has (paraphrase). Jesus rephrased this as, "Love your neighbor as yourself."

This is what I would call the most subtle double-whammy in all scripture.

Whammy #1 – Jesus is urging him to love his neighbors as much as he loves himself. The man triumphantly says, I have done this...I got this. No problem. Oh really, then sell what you have and give it to your neighbor, the poor. The man is cut to the heart because his mindset is still wrong. He clearly loves himself more than others. We often want to change God's laws to say, "Be nice to others," or "Don't be mean." Jesus is saying you are not fulfilling the law just by not being mean, but that you only fulfill the law when you learn how to love and give to those who are in need.

Whammy #2 – Jesus' rephrasing of the tenth commandment was an allusion to the greatest commandment. **Matthew 22:37-39 - "'Love the Lord your God with all your heart and with all your soul and with all your mind.' 38 This is the first and greatest commandment. 39 And the second is like it: 'Love your neighbor as yourself.'**

Jesus appeared to leave out the first four commandments which, paraphrased, tell us we need to always put God first in our lives.

This is why Jesus reminds the young man, "Only God is good." The implication is that he should be seeking to put God first in his life if he wants to enter the Kingdom of Heaven. Then Jesus invites him to do so in asking him to sell all he has and follow Him.

Jesus gave him an opportunity to succeed and he could have done it. However, his running away sad revealed what was really in his heart. He wasn't willing to love God with ALL of his heart, mind, soul, and strength. He loved his personal comfort more than God. He also loved his personal comfort more than helping others.

So what was Jesus getting at? God isn't interested in you just doing things out of obligation. He wants us to love Him and be close to Him all the time. That's what God is truly after. If we are in right relationship with God, all these other things will follow. When God is first, doing what God asks us to do will come more naturally to us. It doesn't mean God won't challenge you from time to time. In fact, I believe if you are giving yourself fully to God, He will be throwing some pretty big challenges your way.

Matthew 6:33 - But seek first his kingdom and his righteousness, and all these things will be given to you as well.

What God is looking for is to see how much of ourselves we are willing to give Him. This is how God was challenging me then and is still challenging me now. I need to put Him first in my life, for He is trustworthy! He is faithful! He will never let me down!

Giving up our old lives can be hard and sometimes it may even seem to be impossible, but God does not ask us to do the impossible. He asks us to give ourselves to Him and THEN with Him all things become possible.

CHAPTER 14

The Calling Comes – God's Purpose and Direction

I learned that the Lord wanted me to be a faithful giver. I was giving my tithe to the church and giving to other ministries as the Lord led me. I was striving to be faithful to God. I wasn't perfect at it but was slowly doing better. Meanwhile, I continued praying for God to reveal His plan for my life.

During that time I was also giving God my time and attention. I was faithful in my Bible study. I was reading it every night when I got home from work and writing down what I was learning or questions I had about what I was reading.

Then it started.

I began having these experiences. As I would be doing my Bible study, I would stand up and just start preaching on whatever scripture I was reading. I was doing this in the middle of my apartment; however, in my mind, I saw myself standing in front of a church preaching to a congregation.

This didn't just happen once, or every once in a while, but it became a regular thing. I was nervous because in my heart I knew God was answering my prayer asking Him to show me what He wanted me to do. But I did not think for one moment that God would ask me to preach. I thought maybe He would ask me to help with the youth group or perhaps do some good deeds in town, or possibly one day teach a Bible study.

One day, I finally broke down and shared with my pastor what was going on. I remember being nervous about it. I thought he would look at me like I was some delusional lunatic. After all, who was I to preach to anyone?

As I shared with him, he had a smile on his face. When I had finished baring this absurd (in my mind) vision with him he boldly said, "Chad, you are getting your call to ministry. Are you going to answer it?"

He went on to explain that I would need to go back to school and receive a proper education and go on to seminary. Now, I thought he was the delusional lunatic. If only this man knew that I wasn't that good of a student. I still don't know how I graduated high school. After high school, I went to a community college for less than a semester and dropped out.

Besides that I did not have the funds to go to college, I didn't have a car; I just could not see a way. At this time, online education was just being birthed, and most schools did not have this as an option.

All I know is that it seemed impossible from my perspective, and I was a bit scared of the implications. I was much like Moses when he got his call to lead Israel.

Exodus 3:9-14 [9] And now the cry of the Israelites has reached me, and I have seen the way the Egyptians are oppressing them.[10] So now, go. I am sending you to Pharaoh to bring my people the Israelites out of Egypt."

[11] But Moses said to God, "Who am I that I should go to Pharaoh and bring the Israelites out of Egypt?"

12 And God said, "I will be with you. And this will be the sign to you that it is I who have sent you: When you have brought the people out of Egypt, you will worship God on this mountain."

13 Moses said to God, "Suppose I go to the Israelites and say to them, 'The God of your fathers has sent me to you,' and they ask me, 'What is his name?' Then what shall I tell them?"

14 God said to Moses, "I AM WHO I AM. This is what you are to say to the Israelites: 'I AM has sent me to you.'"

Exodus 4:1 - Moses answered, "What if they do not believe me or listen to me and say, 'The LORD did not appear to you'?"

Exodus 4:10 - Moses said to the LORD, "Pardon your servant, Lord. I have never been eloquent, neither in the past nor since you have spoken to your servant. I am slow of speech and tongue."

Exodus 4:13 - But Moses said, "Pardon your servant, Lord. Please send someone else."

I was like Moses and many other biblical figures. I was looking at all the reasons why I couldn't and shouldn't do this.

Who am I that I should...

Suppose I go and no one believes You sent me?

But I'm not a good speaker.

And finally, let's get to the bottom line. *Lord, please send someone else!*

I had been praying for God to reveal to me what His will was for my life. I was asking God to give me something to work on. Yet, when

He gave it to me I started back peddling. I was tied up in knots as I considered what this meant and what I should do.

I decided to take a little vacation to see my brother who was living in Colorado Springs at the time. It's interesting, although I was living hand to mouth, the Lord had also encouraged me to start saving money equal to what I was tithing. So I was doing my best to set aside $20 a week. Because I had been faithful at doing that, I had the money I needed to go on this trip.

I didn't realize it at the time but that, in itself, was a financial miracle for me. I had saved money and I hadn't blown it on drugs or alcohol. VICTORY!!!!!!

While I spent time visiting with my brother and his family, I took some personal time alone. I rented a hotel room near Garden of the Gods (I had intended to camp out, but the bitter cold quickly changed my mind). I went there daily and spent time in prayer asking God to help me be sure this was really what He was asking me to do and not some delusional thought running through my brain.

At the end of this time, I knew. I was sure in my heart that this was from the Lord. I didn't know how this was going to unfold; I just knew that Jesus was asking me, like those first disciples, to leave my fishing nets behind and follow Him. No turning back.

I returned to Texas with a purpose. I was going to answer my call to ministry. Now, more than ever, I needed to guard myself against temptation and be more conscientious of what I was doing. I needed to pay attention to the example I was setting by my behavior.

I went to my pastor and told him I was ready to answer my call to ministry and asked him what I should do. He suggested that I look into going to a small junior college about an hour away that was a part of our denomination. They had a church careers department. He thought this would get me going on the right track.

I shared my plan with my dad. Though he is not a Christian, he was very supportive. My dad took me to the college so that I could apply for entry as a student and apply for a job on campus.

I was denied the campus job on the spot. In the interview, I had been honest about my past and that I did not have a long sobriety track. That was a little depressing and was definitely discouraging. I had hoped that this was the way that God was going to provide for me to be able to go to school and work and stay afloat.

During this time, I started sharing with others about my commitment to head back to school to become a pastor. My sharing was met with mixed responses. Looking back now, I can't say that I blame anyone who had doubts about my commitment to my new found faith. Certainly I had started many things that I hadn't finished in my life. Honestly, I had some doubts myself. Not so much about God, but more so about whether or not I would be able to follow through on this commitment.

As I was applying for financial aid, the school's admission department sent me information stating that I had some "financial issues" which I would need to take care of before I could receive any financial assistance. One issue was with the IRS. I also needed to take care of a couple of old debts.

The old Chad would have probably given up by now. I didn't get the job I was hoping for. I was told I needed to take care of my debts which I did not have money to take care of, and I still had no vision for how any of this could succeed. However, I kept hearing in my head and in my heart to keep going and to trust the Lord.

I called the IRS (with some fear and trembling) and the creditors to make arrangements to pay what I owed. I began chipping away at it, all the while being faithful to God with my tithe. Because of the debts I was paying on, I did not have enough to live off of and continue to save money as I had before. I was in a serious financial tight spot. It seemed like the harder I worked to do things the right way, the harder things got.

I often questioned how the financial side of things was going to work out. In my eyes, it wasn't going to. I secretly believed that I would pursue this and it would end up failing. But one thing I committed to was being faithful in the pursuit of answering this call.

I was doing what I knew to do. I would like to share with you, if you're not sure what to do, do what you KNOW you need to do. Take one step at a time. My problem is that I couldn't see how I was going to get there. I kept looking at what I didn't have. However, God was just asking me to have faith in Him and to keep taking the next step.

Moses didn't know all the obstacles he would have to face; he just knew that God was in charge, and his job was to be faithful. Like Moses, I did not do everything right during this time, but when I messed up I learned to admit it, confess it to the Lord, repent, and get back on track.

I was chipping away at my debts and every time I had an opportunity to take another step toward the vision God had given me, I'd act on it. One of the greatest blessings you can gain in your life is being committed to the destination.

Romans 5

Therefore, since we have been justified through faith, we have peace with God through our Lord Jesus Christ, [2] through whom we have gained access by faith into this grace in which we now stand. And we boast in the hope of the glory of God. [3] Not only so, but we also glory in our sufferings, because we know that suffering produces perseverance; [4] perseverance, character; and character, hope. [5] And hope does not put us to shame, because God's love has been poured out into our hearts through the Holy Spirit, who has been given to us.

God was helping me grow and mature as I was going through this process. He was teaching me to persevere through the hard times instead of quitting as I had in the past. He was building up my character as a man of God, and giving me an opportunity to experience His goodness as I went through the difficulties. I can testify from experience that when we put our hope in the Lord our hope is never put to shame.

Once I was committed to the destination, the decision making (the war of reasoning within my mind) was already a battle that had been fought and won. Now all there was, was to do. Do what I knew to do and then wait until the next step presented itself.

Even while I was waiting for the next step, I was preparing myself to move to college. I started looking at my possessions and knew I needed to trim down my belongings because I couldn't take them all with me. Plus, I needed the money. So I started selling my stuff.

Whenever I sold something, I tithed on whatever I sold. There were a couple of relatives that sent me money to help me out. I tithed on what they gifted me. Then one day out of the blue, I received a check from someone I had only met once through a friend in Dallas. She mailed me a check for $300 with a note encouraging me to be faithful. I knew that was God moving to provide for me through the generosity of others. I remember crying and thanking God for the provision. I tithed on everything I received, not because I didn't need the money; on the contrary, I was still way short of what I needed to go to school, but I just wanted to be faithful in honoring God with everything.

I would later read a book that would help me better understand God's upside down economy. Where we, in this world, gather to receive our provision, God calls us to trust Him and give, and in the right time He will supply all of our needs. That's what happened to me. I kept doing my best to be faithful and God ultimately provided what I needed, and then some.

Two weeks before I was to leave Buffalo to go to school, I finally got a letter from the financial aid office stating that since I had resolved my issue with the IRS I was eligible for student loans. I received enough to cover my first year's tuition, with room and board, but it was not enough for books or money to live on. I was going to have to figure that one out. For the time, I rejoiced in what I had and stayed committed to following the Lord's plan for my life.

The day I was leaving to check into school was a Sunday. I went to church as usual. My pastor shared with the congregation that I was leaving to go to school and they prayed for me. Then the pastor had me stand with him at the door of the church so the members of the congregation could wish me well.

One after another wished me well and shook my hand giving me a "little something to help you out." That church family helped me in ways that I could never repay. They gave me encouragement when I needed it. They provided me opportunities to grow in service. They helped me start following God and blessed me with the resources I needed to get me going.

By the time I left the church that morning, I had enough money to pay for my books and a little spending money left over. Jehovah Jireh – "God is my provider," indeed!

The Lord didn't stop there. Once I got to college, I started looking for work but wasn't having much luck. I shared my plight with my counselor who became a dear friend to me while I was there. Rev. Barberee helped me apply for a scholarship for church careers students. If I remember correctly, it was either a $1,000 or $1250 scholarship. I got the scholarship and when my financial aid arrived at the school, I received a check back from the school for the amount of the scholarship.

This allowed me to focus on my studies without having to get a job. I worked my tail off to make it count. Part of my working so hard was a little bit of a lack of confidence in my own abilities and a lot of fear of failure. A little fear can sometimes be a good thing if it helps us move in the right direction.

CHAPTER 15

God Prepares His Children to Fulfill His Purpose

As I mentioned, I was worried about being able to keep up with college academics, so I studied like my life depended on it. There were two scriptures that stuck with me at that time. No, they didn't just stick with me, they drove me.

Luke 12:48

From everyone who has been given much, much will be demanded; and from the one who has been entrusted with much, much more will be asked.

Galatians 6:7

Do not be deceived: God cannot be mocked. A man reaps what he sows.

I was scared of failing. I had failed so much of my life. I wanted to succeed. I wanted to not just start something, but I wanted to finish it. I knew a real change had happened in me and I wanted it to bear fruit. I was hungry to discover my new identity of who I could be in Christ Jesus.

Philippians 4:13 – I can do all this through him who gives me strength.

This wasn't just scripture; it was alive in me. God's Word was coming to life in me, and I longed to find out who I could be with God. What was my potential?

By the end of my first semester of college, I had quit smoking cigarettes. I finished my first semester with straight A's. I don't think I had ever gotten straight A's before, even in grade school and certainly not in high school.

But there was still something missing in my life. I was lonely. I longed for a godly wife. Temptation was knocking on my door. I was still fairly fresh in my walk. I could have easily messed up everything God was doing for me at that time. Luckily, God talked some sense into me and helped me realize that I needed to be faithful in ALL things, and I needed to guard myself against temptation.

I realized I was having a tough time meeting women my age who were single, Christian women. So I turned to a Christian singles website to see if I could meet some nice Christian women my age to talk to.

At this time internet dating was just getting started. Truthfully I was kind of nervous about it, and I did not want anyone to know I was doing the online dating thing. Part of it was that it was such a new thing I was worried about what people might think. Would they view me as desperate? Would they shun this new way of meeting people because it broke from traditional dating? I talked to a lady or two here and there, but nothing ever seemed to click.

In the meantime, I kept working hard at school, plus I was working toward my calling of being a pastor. Over winter break, a friend of mine, Charles, had just bought himself a new truck and he knew I did not have any transportation. He blessed me incredibly by giving me his car. I couldn't believe it. What a blessing! God was continuing to provide. This blessing was another major piece of the puzzle that God orchestrated that would open up His plan for me. Eventually, it would be the gift that would enable me to meet my wife and would take me to my next stage in life.

When I returned to school with the car, I told Rev. Barberee about it. She celebrated this great gift with me. It was a great gift, not only because of the generous nature of it, but also, because it opened a door of opportunity for me to start preaching at some local area churches. We had known about this opportunity but because I didn't have a car to get to the churches it had seemed unlikely it would work out. Now, this opportunity seemed more than possible; it seemed imminent.

Preparing Me for My Bride

I was continually learning that investing myself into God's Kingdom was one of the wisest decisions I could make. Scripture reminds us that man was not created to live alone.

Genesis 2:15

The LORD God took the man and put him in the Garden of Eden to work it and take care of it.

We were created to live with God first and foremost; to interact with God in His creation, to work in harmony with God and enjoy the world He created for us.

Genesis 2:18

The LORD God said, "It is not good for the man to be alone. I will make a helper suitable for him."

Genesis 2:24

That is why a man leaves his father and mother and is united to his wife, and they become one flesh.

One of the many ways God has blessed us in creation is by making our life more rewarding by having someone to share it with. That's why I believe God created the world and then put us in it. He desired to have a relationship with us so we could mutually enjoy His creation together. Just as we are created in God's image, we also have His desire to live in relationship with others. The Bible tells us God is love, love needs to be expressed, and can only be expressed in relationship with others.

I've already shared that before I gave my life to the Lord, I viewed women from a wrong perspective. I selfishly looked to women to see which of my needs they could fulfill. That's the central theme of sin. Sin tells us to indulge ourselves, to live for our own gratification. I had a wrong understanding of how to relate to women and that needed to be corrected. My view had been very selfish.

In giving my life to God, He began teaching me how to live in a right relationship with Him. He was God; I was not. He has all the right answers; I do not. He is righteous and just, I am not. Only He deserves to sit on the throne of Lordship; I do not. I learned from Jesus that if I want to be in right relationship with God, then I need to develop a servant's heart.

Jesus himself gave the example.

Mark 10:45

For even the Son of Man did not come to be served, but to serve, and to give His life a ransom for many."

Jesus was teaching the disciples, both then and now, that we need to change our perspective. We place way too much value on serving ourselves and not nearly enough on serving others. Learning to put others before myself was a key concept that I had to learn before He could give me a wife and a family.

Had God given me a wife before this it would have been like giving a million dollars to a child with no sense of financial stewardship; I would have wasted this great opportunity and not valued it properly. I had already proven this to myself multiple times in life. I had a lot of growing up to do in learning how to be a good steward of the gifts of God.

In **Ephesians 4:21-24**

when you heard about Christ and were taught in him in accordance with the truth that is in Jesus. [22] You were taught, with regard to your former way of life, to put off your old self, which is being corrupted by its deceitful desires; [23] to be made new in the attitude of your minds; [24] and to put on the new self, created to be like God in true righteousness and holiness.

This change in character is what the Lord was helping me do. I was learning to put off the old self and put on the new self. In this case, it was changing my desire for women from being a lustful, flesh-pleasing desire to serve my needs, to desiring a wholesome, mutually beneficial, and fulfilling relationship.

Ephesians 5:25-33

Husbands, love your wives, just as Christ loved the church and gave himself up for her [26] to make her holy, cleansing her by the washing with water through the word, [27] and to present her to himself as a radiant church, without stain or wrinkle or any other blemish, but holy and blameless. [28] In this same way, husbands ought to love their wives as their own bodies. He who loves his wife loves himself. [29] After all, no one ever hated their own body, but they feed and care for their body, just as Christ does the church— [30] for we are members of his body.[31] "For this reason a man will leave his father and mother and be united to his wife, and the two will become one flesh." [32] This is a profound mystery—but I am talking about Christ and the church. [33] However, each one of

you also must love his wife as he loves himself, and the wife must respect her husband.

I thank the Lord every day that He spent time preparing me before He gave me my wife. I'm sure she thanks the Lord every day for that also. Especially since she probably sees my imperfections more than anyone else.

The Lord was putting my life in order. He was helping me grow in understanding of how to love my future wife. He also taught me that the respect I desired as a man would flow naturally from my wife if I loved her properly.

God had a lot of work to do in me before I would be ready to meet my wife.

__√__ Give life to the Lord
__√__ Quit using alcohol and drugs
__√__ Get a proper view of women
__√__ Learn to handle money properly
__√__ Quit smoking
__√__ Be committed to doing the Lord's work
__√__ Get transportation
__√__ Be honest about who you are and what you are looking for in a wife

God was preparing me for my bride.

CHAPTER 16

Finding My Pearl

Matthew 13:45-46

[45] "Again, the kingdom of heaven is like a merchant looking for fine pearls. [46] When he found one of great value, he went away and sold everything he had and bought it.

Obviously, this text is speaking of the pearl of great price as the Kingdom of Heaven. When we find the Kingdom of Heaven, it asks us how we are going to respond. Are we going to give up our other treasures (our worldly values) and invest ourselves in the Kingdom of God?

However, there is another principle at work here that lends itself to other areas. The principle being when you find someone you love, what will you be willing to do to be with them?

I had been praying for a godly woman, someone who had a strong walk with the Lord and who was faithful to Him. This was very important to me as I began looking for my "Pearl of Great Price." I needed a woman who could talk with me about our love for the Lord and who desired to raise children to know the Lord.

I was in my early 30s and wanted a family. I didn't want to waste time with women who did not fit what I was looking for. I was pretty specific as I began searching for this great treasure who would bless me by becoming my wife.

Rene and I were both 33 years old when we met each other online through a Christian singles dating website. She was in the small town of Lincoln, KS and I was in Jacksonville, TX attending Lon Morris College. In a way, being so far apart geographically was a good thing. We spent a ton of time talking to each other over the internet and the phone. We really got to know each other without the physical temptations.

As I mentioned, I was pretty specific in what I was looking for in a wife and brought that to the forefront in my conversations. I wanted to separate the wheat from the chaff. So I was probably a little more forward than one might normally be.

As Rene and I began talking to one another, I was grateful to find out she was a long-time Christian. She was a modest woman who although beautiful did not view herself as such. She was a non-drinker, non-smoker and desired to have a godly husband. She wanted a relationship where she and her husband would honor the Lord in how they lived and how they raised their kids.

She was exactly the woman I was looking for. Except she didn't play the piano... because you know, everyone expects the pastor's wife to play the piano. :o)

I thank the Lord that He helped me quit smoking before meeting Rene. Our profiles asked if we preferred a non-smoker which we both marked. We would not have crossed each other's paths if I had not quit. Praise God for helping me take on new healthy habits which prepared me in time to meet my "Pearl of Great Price."

I didn't waste much time or beat around the bush. She was the woman I had been looking for. I let her know pretty quickly that I was looking for a wife. I told her about my sordid past and that I had hepatitis C. I figured if I was going to scare her off, I might as well scare her off sooner rather than later, she was either the right woman, or she wasn't. I didn't consider the third option, that she might be crazy.

I decided to be bold and truthful about what I wanted and to trust that God was guiding both of us. I prayed daily for her and for God's guidance. I asked the Lord if this was who He had chosen for me. If so, let it be, if not, I asked the Lord to let that be revealed also. How I didn't scare her off is still amazing to me. All I can say is she was definitely trusting the Lord, a lot!

As I said earlier, we were both praying to the Lord to give us guidance. I was being bold, and she sought God's direction. I had asked her within a few days if she could ever see herself leaving Kansas. After all, I was working on my call to ministry and going to school in Texas. If this did work out, was she willing to move?

She was a bit caught off guard and probably gave the best answer she could at the time. I think she said something like, "Well, I guess if the Lord was leading me."

When we finished talking that night, she turned to God in prayer and asked God to speak to her through the Word which was her habit. God spoke to her heart and reminded her that a wife must leave and cleave to her husband. Rene was taken aback by this because the thought of actually marrying me had not been on her mind as a serious option. After the Lord had said that to her the thought was there, and she was open to seeing where the Lord might lead us.

Before meeting Rene online I had applied for, and won, a scholarship to go to South Korea to study at a university over the summer. It was all expenses paid, the plane tickets had been bought, tuition was paid, and I had gotten my passport and was set to spend most of the summer studying abroad.

When I met Rene online, it was getting close to the end of the academic school year. I knew I was going to be spending most of the summer in Korea, but I wanted to meet Rene face to face. I saw an opportunity; there was a short break in classes around Easter.

When Rene and I tell the story of our meeting and getting married within three months, we always seem to tell the story a little differently from one another. But one thing is always the same. We both firmly believe God brought us together.

Rene and I had talked about marriage before we ever saw one another face to face. Since we had already talked about the possibility of getting married, I wanted to see her in person. I asked about coming to visit her. I can only imagine how nervous she was. To my amazement, she said yes, as long as I would agree to stay at her parent's house. I agreed and the rest is history.

We were already discussing marriage before I went out to meet her face to face for the first time. When I left from meeting her, I was certain she was the one. I didn't want to wait and hem-haw around. I wanted this Pearl of Great Price named Rene to be my bride. I was all in for her and still am.

We got married a couple of months later, just before I left for Korea. We spent a couple of weeks together as newlyweds, then I went to Korea and returned about eight weeks later. We had another couple of weeks together before I returned to Texas to finish my associate's degree. After that, I moved to Kansas to finish my bachelor's degree so we could live near her family while I finished school.

If I had not had God in my life, Rene and I would not have gotten married. Nor would our lives be as fulfilling as they are today. God preparing me ahead of time and helping me to find my Pearl in Rene is just one of many ways God blesses those who seek to honor Him with their lives.

Romans 8:28 –

And we know that in all things God works for the good of those who love him, who have been called according to his purpose.

Because God was the focus and in the forefront of our discussions, I think it gave both of us a certain comfort that although we were certainly moving quickly with our marriage, it just felt right. I believe God was answering my prayers in giving me Rene as my wife. Hopefully, I would be the answer to her prayers as well.

Not only did God bless us by giving us each other but God has continued to provide for us, protect us, and bless us. God has provided us with work, blessed us with two children, kept us safe and allowed us to continue growing as His children through the ministries He has allowed us to be a part of. We continue to see His blessings in our lives.

Rene and I have both had to (or should I say get to) learn what it means to love one another sacrificially. It was tough in the beginning because Rene and I were both very independent people. We had to learn to talk to one another so we could be on the same page. We learned to compromise and how to set aside what we wanted to do for the sake of our whole family.

God has been teaching us a lot about the joys of sacrificial love. We see how loving each other this way enriches our relationship and our lives. We don't do this perfectly, and I'm sure we will be stretched to grow in this area more in the near future, but we don't do so begrudgingly. Every time I make a sacrifice for the sake of our family I somehow get blessed, usually in the form of love and respect from my wife which I value highly. There's nothing like loving those who love you.

I have seen Rene make even more sacrifices than I feel I have made. As a result, I continue to grow more deeply in love with her as I see how much she gives of herself for me, for our kids, and for others. Every time I see her go out of her way for me, it makes me want to go more out of my way for her.

I would never have had such a rewarding family life if it were not for having Jesus in my life. Jesus is continuing to teach me to love her as He loves the church (meaning His body of believers – not the building or the denomination).

Think about what I just shared for a moment. The more sacrifices I see Rene make for the kids and me, the more I want to make sacrifices for her. Now think about that in your relationship with Christ. The more God sees us learning to love Him and love others sacrificially, the more God desires to do for you.

As Galatians 6:7 says,

Do not be deceived: God cannot be mocked. A man reaps what he sows.

This scripture is God encouraging us. If you want to get God's best in your life, then give God your best. If you do, you will come to experience the awesome presence of God in many ways. It will become your testimony so you can share with others about God's goodness bearing fruit in your life.

However, the opposite is true also. If you don't intentionally make time for God in your life, then you will not see God at work in your life. It's your choice. Unfortunately, too many people don't take the time to give God their best.

Yes, I met my wife on the internet. Two people in a sea of billions. We were drawn to one another by God because we were both seeking God's will for our lives. We believed God was at the center of both of our lives, and we were seeking God's guidance in our relationship, so we had the confidence to act quickly when the Lord opened the door.

This relationship is similar to my relationship with the Lord. The longer I am in this relationship, the more I love them both. It doesn't mean everything is easy for us. It just means that we are committed to working through whatever comes our way together, with God at the center.

CHAPTER 17

Growing in Ministry

So by the end of my first year of school, I was engaged to be married. I was preaching regularly and was scheduled to be assigned to be the preacher at two small country churches when I returned from summer break.

I came back to Texas with focus. I wanted to finish my associate's degree by December so I could move to Kansas and be with my wife. I was also looking forward to serving these two small country churches as a pastor and beginning to fulfill my call to ministry.

I had no idea at the time that when God allowed me to serve these churches He was preparing me for a major change in my life. He was giving me the experience of serving people that I did not share a lot in common with which began preparing me for my move to Kansas. After all, they were country folk, and I was from the big city (having lived in Dallas and Houston most of my life).

I applied to a college in Kansas where I could complete my bachelor's degree. I was accepted to Kansas Wesleyan University in Salina, KS.

During the Thanksgiving break, I came to Kansas to be with my wife. I had already been talking with the District Superintendent (DS) who had appointed me to serve the two churches in Texas. He called Salina and spoke to the DS there to let him know I would be moving up there and had been doing well for him in Texas.

When I got to Kansas, I met with the DS. After spending some time sharing with him my call to ministry and the path I was taking to get to seminary, he shared with me about an opportunity. There was a church in Ellsworth, Kansas, where a pastor was going on an extended leave due to health issues. He told me that he needed someone to serve as pastor from the end of the year until the end of June. God's handwriting was all over this.

During the Thanksgiving break, Rene and I were able to have a meeting with a committee from the church. They knew I did not have a lot of experience, especially in comparison to the more seasoned pastors they were used to having. All I could do was share my heart for doing the Lord's will and my desire to serve Him well. As I shared my heart with them, they reciprocated and accepted Rene and me.

I have to say serving the church in Ellsworth for six months did more to help me grow in my understanding of my call to love the people I serve than I could ever have imagined. I often look back and feel they served me more than I served them. I still have a deep affection in my heart for them.

The six months of serving that congregation gave me a lot of ministry opportunities. From visiting a young man in jail that I would have contact with for years to come, to visiting with a young lady who was trying to find her way in life. I had some ministry opportunities with the youth of that church, and even some one-on-one time with several of the members of the church that was mutually beneficial.

In short, God gave me a season of loving a congregation. In return, I received a season of being loved by a congregation. It was pretty awesome, and I am so thankful that I still have opportunities (though limited) to enjoy my walk with the Lord with these fine, kind, loving and generous people.

While this time of walking in love was blessed, it made what was about to happen so much more difficult.

Sometimes God says No.

The end of June was on the horizon. The Ellsworth church still needed a pastor and to my joy they wanted Rene and me to continue there. We wanted to continue there as well. However, it was not God's plan for us.

This was one of those times where you pray for something and God's answer is no. No is rarely a pleasant answer to receive when you truly desire a yes.

I believe it was sometime in March when one of the congregation members, Ken, asked the DS if the church could keep me as their pastor. The DS did not beat around the bush and told him no. He reminded Ken and later reminded me, that this appointment was a temporary one. To tell you the truth, I think both the congregation and myself were pretty disappointed. No, more like frustrated.

It just didn't seem to make sense at the time. The answers we were given were logical, but they did not appear to be led by God. They appeared more to be led by policies and systems. The key words here are, "appeared to be."

I think we all have times in life where we judge what is happening by appearance and in doing so, we question the decisions of others and whether or not they are in line with the will of God. We also question whether or not God is answering our prayers because He doesn't answer them the way we want Him to.

Consider Balaam and King Balak.

Numbers 22-24

In summary of the story of Balaam, we see a diviner (Balaam) who, in my opinion, God is trying to transform into a prophet. I believe God is always trying to transform people to meet their potential. Balaam is like many who seek the Lord. There is a certain authenticity to our desire to be fully committed to God. However, our fallen humanity often gets in the way. God is always seeking to lead us into His ways and transform us for the better.

Balaam starts with good intentions. When he is given an offer from a worldly king (Balak, King of Moab) to serve him for great financial gain Balaam instead of rejoicing at his great fortune, goes to God to ask for counsel.

Balak requested that Balaam put a curse on Israel by using sorcery. All Balak wanted was for Balaam to do his will and he would be rewarded handsomely. Balak did not ask Balaam what God's will was nor did he seek to find if there was anything he could do to gain God's favor. Like Balak, sometimes we want to be king of our own lands, we want everything to function the way we imagine it should. We rarely stop to consider whether or not we are thinking about things properly or if what we are doing is truly God's desire.

Balaam starts by seeking the God of Israel. Balaam had heard how Israel's God was strong and the secret of their success. Balaam was wise enough to think to himself that he needed to know the will of the God of Israel so he could rightly discern what, and how, he should respond to the request.

Balaam returns to Balak's entourage to tell them he cannot fulfill their request. God was for Israel, and there was nothing he could do that would change that. Isn't that great news? There is nothing someone else can do to you to keep God's blessings and protection from you once He has chosen you.

Key words here, *there is nothing someone else can do,* to remove God's blessings from you. There are, however, things you can do to move outside of God's blessing and protection. This is what Balaam, and later Israel, were about to find out.

Balaam started well. He started by telling King Balak's messengers that he could not do as the king had asked because God's blessing was upon them. Balaam did as God asked and sent the messengers home to the king with that message.

King Balak did not want to receive the message and instead, he tried to force his will upon Balaam. Balak believed if he just offered more money to Balaam he'd change his mind.

Another time princes, very wealthy and influential men, came to Balaam. Balaam already knew what the Lord's answer was. We know this because he tells the men right away (Numbers 22:18) that even if they had all the silver and gold in the world he still would not do what they were asking. Had he left it at that, I think God would have been well pleased with Balaam.

However, Balaam caved into their pressure. He said, let me see if perhaps there is something he misunderstood or if perhaps the Lord has changed his mind.

I believe this is what caused God to send His angel to block the road when Balaam tried to go to Moab. God was trying to help Balaam see that he was on a treacherous path by not accepting what the Lord had said the first time. A path just as treacherous as Balak's.

Luckily, Balaam was ready to learn from his mistakes and asked for forgiveness from the Lord. Balak, however, had no humility and could not accept God's answer. The further he tried to push his own will, the more trouble he heaped upon himself.

The reason for sharing the story of Balaam and Balak is that I believe sometimes we get our perspective mixed up and assume God is always going to answer our prayers the way we want him to, with a yes. God does promise to answer prayer, in His way and time. But sometimes His answer is no. Sometimes, if we seek to understand God's will and then change our desires to match God's will, we find the blessings He desires to give us.

I wonder what would have happened if when Balak heard the message of God's blessing upon Israel he had changed his own heart and sought to bless Israel in line with God's will?

Scripture gives us the answer.

Genesis 12:3

3 I will bless those who bless you, and whoever curses you I will curse; and all peoples on earth will be blessed through you."

Balak could have brought himself in line with the will of God and received a blessing for doing so. Unfortunately, Balak unwittingly chose to be cursed by fighting against the will of God.

Luke 11:9-13

9 "So I say to you: Ask and it will be given to you; seek and you will find; knock and the door will be opened to you. 10 For everyone who asks receives; the one who seeks finds; and to the one who knocks, the door will be opened.

11 "Which of you fathers, if your son asks for[a] a fish, will give him a snake instead? 12 Or if he asks for an egg, will give him a scorpion? 13 If you then, though you are evil, know how to give good gifts to your children, how much more will your Father in heaven give the Holy Spirit to those who ask him!"

Here's the real issue, in my opinion. Do you trust God? Do you trust God's wisdom, His character, His love? Do you trust that God desires good things for you? What parent does not desire good things for their children? Only an evil parent would not want what's best for their child. Is God evil that He would not desire to give us His best? Absolutely NOT!!!!

The real issue is we need to seek to be in God's will and trust that He will move in our lives in such a way as to bring us to the better things He desires to give us. This is the lesson I was going to learn from this experience.

Although in my heart, and in the hearts of many of the church's congregation members we were a good fit (and I still believe that because our love is still strong after all these years) God had a plan in moving Rene and me.

God moved us to serve a church in Mentor, Kansas. If God had not moved us to the Mentor church, I would not have come to find the Salina Rescue Mission. Looking back now, I feel kind of like a schmuck. Remember how Israel complained when they were going through the wilderness to the Promised Land? That was me. I was so busy complaining that I failed to see what God was doing.

Rene and I moved into our next phase as pastor and wife, and she soon gave birth to our first child, Jeremiah. God provided for me through the Mentor church and taught me many valuable lessons about ministry, about people, and about myself.

I have to say, I made several mistakes as a pastor there. I thought a little too highly of myself and I alienated myself from a few congregation members. I can say I had good intentions, but sometimes I just missed the mark.

Now I say all that and it probably sounds like things were a disaster, but I wouldn't go that far because there were several good things that happened there. I met a lot of good people. I developed some good relationships that Rene and I still maintain today. God was able to use me to help a few people work through some issues they were struggling with, but God deserves the credit for that, not me.

Two significant things came out of our time in Mentor. One was that I started to get a better understanding of my call to ministry. I realized that my call was not to pastor a church, so much as it was to reach lost and hurting people. My call was to "be" the church in the community, reaching out to people who were in need.

This call led me to look around the community of Salina to find out about the different helping agencies there. That way, when I came across people who needed help I would know of some resources to connect them with. My desire to help people in need led me to the second significant thing that came out of my time in Mentor. I found out about the Salina Rescue Mission.

CHAPTER 18

Growing to Understand God's Call

When I first came to the Salina Rescue Mission I did not know much about the place. I had heard that it was a men's homeless shelter which some people referred to it as the Gospel Mission. I don't remember all the details from the first time I visited, but I do remember talking to their Development Director, Eric Frank, and then to the Executive Director, Steve Kmetz.

As I met with these men, each shared information about the Mission with me. They shared different aspects of what they did and ways for people to get involved volunteering at the Mission. What was very evident, and what got me excited about the Salina Rescue Mission was that they were a ministry who understood they were the church, and their mission was to help lost, needy, and hurting people. They did this by providing food, shelter, clothing, and meeting other basic needs, and by teaching the rehabilitative teachings of the Lord Jesus Christ.

For me, it was the complete package. They provided practical help immediately to people who were struggling. The shelter could house up to 85 men (a different agency offers women and children shelter across town). They also served hot, nutritious meals to anyone in the community. People who came for a meal did not have to be staying at the shelter. Anyone who was hungry could come for a free meal. No one ever had to prove their need, all they had to do was show up.

Additionally, the Mission offered free clothing (both for shelter guests and to any man in the community who was in need). They provided showers, laundry services, toiletries, and over the counter medicines. They provided assistance to those who qualified for aid to see a doctor and helped with the purchase of many prescription medications (as long as they fit within their guidelines). And they did it all in the name of Jesus. The name of Jesus is lifted up daily at the Mission at their evening chapel service. The Mission required guests [they do not refer to men as clients but as guests] and visitors who came for the evening meal to attend chapel. This concept is what hooked me. The ministry understood that while people were coming to them to get their basic physical needs met, they also had an opportunity to address spiritual needs. This was the type of help that could change a person's life forever.

To live life successfully we need to know our origin and our purpose for living. We need direction for living that only the Lord can provide. The Lord had changed my life by teaching me His lessons, and this is the help the Mission continues to offer men.

The Mission understood my journey and helped me discover some deeper truths about the journey I had been on. I had tried many times to get my life together and had always failed because I was trying to live life on my terms, without God. It wasn't until I surrendered control over my life to the Lord and started doing my best to live my life on God's terms that I found the peace, direction, and a sense of purpose that I had been missing.

While standing in the Mission learning what all they did to help people in need, my sense of purpose was being called in a new direction. God had gotten me this far, and was now about to launch me onto the next part of my journey.

I volunteered at the Salina Rescue Mission for the next two years. I spoke at chapel services, visited with the shelter guests, and started teaching a class for the New Life Program (a long-term discipleship program that focuses on helping men find their lives in Christ). I also started building relationships with the staff.

Steve and I would meet and share with each other where we were in our journey. Scott McDaniel (who was the New Life Program Director at that time) became a good friend, and we challenged one another to grow a deeper understanding of the men we were working with. Bob Highgate, one of the shelter supervisors, was a great encourager who made every volunteer feel needed and valued.

During my time volunteering at the Mission, I remember telling Steve and Scott that I needed to take a break from my volunteer work because I was starting seminary. I was going to be driving from Mentor to Kansas City every Sunday night and returning on Thursday. Thursday through Sunday needed to be time for me to spend with my family, do my homework and reading from school, fulfill my pastoral responsibilities, and take care of whatever else came up before I headed back off for school.

I remember sinking into a sort of depression during that time. Things were not going the way I thought they should at the church. I was not too happy with the denominational seminary I was attending, and I was starting to feel burned out. My wife was also affected. While she had a husband, most of the time she was a single parent.

My wife and I sat down and started talking about how we were feeling. We both knew something had to give. I had finished my Bachelor of Arts in Religion at Kansas Wesleyan University but was facing four years of seminary to get the Master of Divinity degree that our denomination required for those looking to become a fully ordained elder. This was early in year one of my seminary endeavor and we were already feeling the stress and unhealthiness of the road we were on. We knew something needed to change for our family's sake and our spiritual well-being.

There were two things the Lord gave me to help me through this time. One was that He gave me a group of brothers at the seminary. I could talk to them and share, in a very transparent way, what I was going through. We met weekly and talked to each other regularly throughout the week. This was nothing short of a blessing from heaven. Eric, John, Keith, Ben, Alberto, and Jamie were faithful friends and accountability partners, and we formed a covenant with one another. Later Jose, Richard, and Rusty, would also become a part of this brotherhood.

The second thing the Lord gave me to help me through this was the Mission. I was feeling the stress of living four days a week out of town going to seminary and trying to pack into three days all my sermon prep, pastoral responsibilities, and homework. I felt like I was giving my family my leftovers. During this time, I started missing the volunteer work I had been doing at the Mission. After talking to my wife about this, she agreed that perhaps going back to volunteering at the Mission would help in some way.

I know that seems illogical. I was already stretched too thin, but there is something about doing what God calls you to do that, in itself, becomes a reward.

Isaiah 40:30-31

Even youths grow tired and weary, and young men stumble and fall; [31] but those who hope in the LORD will renew their strength. They will soar on wings like eagles; they will run and not grow weary, they will walk and not be faint.

As I returned to my volunteer work, I started to feel rejuvenated. I felt joy enter back into my life, like a wave of fresh air. It energized me and drove me. I felt like I was making a difference. God was calling me to help others and in the process of doing what God asked me to do, God blessed me. God met me at my point of need when I surrendered to Him, despite the appearance that I didn't have the time.

When we are doing God's will, He has a way of making sure we have what we need to continue. For me, I found the peace and rejuvenation I needed to keep going forward.

CHAPTER 19

Discerning God's Lead

During September and October of 2006, Rene and I had several discussions about seminary and the church we were serving. We both felt that we needed a change. We prayed earnestly to the Lord for direction. We asked the Lord if what we were feeling was a part of His will to help us move into the next season, or if this was growing pains we just had to go through as a life lesson to be learned. Rene and I both felt we needed to explore our options and continued to pray for God to lead us.

A major part of this searching related to my seminary education. I wanted to explore Asbury Theological Seminary in Kentucky. They had a great reputation but were several states away from where we lived. As part of our discernment process, we wanted to visit the school to find out what the seminary was like in person. We made arrangements and went on an exploratory journey to Kentucky.

Rene and I prayed as we went there and prayed throughout the trip. We met with some students, toured the school, met with faculty, and went to a worship service on campus. We also met with a district superintendent from our denomination about the possibility of getting assigned to a church in the area while attending seminary. Everything about the trip was very positive. We felt a kindred spirit with the atmosphere of the school and the connections we made with the both the students and the professors.

Rene and I both left with a firm sense that this was the kind of seminary I should be attending because it appeared to be a great fit for us. We were asking if there was a better place for us to be and the answer for us seemed to be yes. However, little did we know that while this seemed like a good fit, it was not God's plan for us.

Rene and I continued praying after we got home. Our prayer at this point was no longer if Asbury was a better fit for me. Instead, our prayers were focused on us being in God's will. Being in God's will, even in a place that feels uncomfortable, is better than being in a comfortable place that is not God's will.

We prayed often. The prayer was something like, "Lord, if this is Your will for us then bless it. Open the doors and sweep away all the stumbling blocks and remove the obstacles. If this is not Your will, then please close the door and direct us where You would have us go."

During the next few months, I did what I knew to do. I finished the application process to Asbury and was accepted. We shared with our district superintendent our desire for change. We let him know that when our appointed time was complete, we were considering a move to Kentucky. We also shared this with the congregation we were serving. We had great peace about letting the church, and our DS, know of the plans for change. We just didn't know at that point that God had other plans.

When we had met with the district superintendent in Kentucky it was a very positive meeting. He appeared to be optimistic that he would be able to find a church that would be a fit for our family. He encouraged me to stay in touch with him, which I did. About once a month I would contact him and remind him of our family, our desire to serve, and to see if there was anything he needed from us.

Every time we talked, he would encourage me, saying he believed he would have an appointment and would encourage me to call him back next month. Our church appointment ended in June, and that is when we were planning to move.

November came and went as did December. In January, and again in February, we continued to call the district superintendent as we continued to pray for God to bless this if it was His will, or block it if it was not. When March came, the district superintendent stated that he did not have a church yet. At this point, his tone changed from being optimistic to one of uncertainty.

I have to confess; my prayers started to change. I began to pray longer prayers and with greater intensity. My prayer life was blossoming under the stress of uncertainty. Isn't that how it usually works? When we're confident and comfortable our prayers tend to be short. A quick, "Thanks God and help old so-and-so out." But when stress, concerns, health issues, financial issues, or family issues arise we pull out our prayer carpet and draw as close to the Lord as we can.

Consider Jonah

Jonah heard the voice of God calling him to a specific ministry. He was called to go to Nineveh and preach a message of repentance. Instead of doing what God called him to do, he ran in the opposite direction. God called him to travel across land heading in a northeast direction. Jonah went to the sea and traveled across water heading west.

Jonah was content to run from God. But God sent a storm to help Jonah change direction. The storm helped Jonah consider his personal dependence on God, accept the conviction that what he was doing was against God, and then the storm turned into a blessing to help Jonah reconcile with God. As everyone on the ship began to pray to their gods for help in the storm, Jonah did not. Why? Jonah knew in his heart why God had sent the storm. Jonah knew he was in rebellion against God's will.

When Jonah was asked why he wasn't praying, Jonah thought there was no point in praying. He thought God would not listen to his prayers because he knew he had defied God. This is where Jonah and many other people get it wrong. Just because you enter into a season of rebellion against God, it does not mean that God won't have anything to do with you ever again.

Time and time again in the Bible, the Lord sends His Word to tell His people to return to Him.

Deuteronomy 30:1-4

When all these blessings and curses I have set before you come on you and you take them to heart wherever the LORD your God disperses you among the nations, [2] and when you and your children return to the LORD your God and obey him with all your heart and with all your soul according to everything I command you today, [3] then the LORD your God will restore your fortunes and have compassion on you and gather you again from all the nations where he scattered you. [4] Even if you have been banished to the most distant land under the heavens, from there the LORD your God will gather you and bring you back.

Jeremiah 3:12

Go, proclaim this message toward the north: "'Return, faithless Israel,' declares the LORD, 'I will frown on you no longer, for I am faithful,' declares the LORD, 'I will not be angry forever.

Jeremiah 24:7

[7] I will give them a heart to know me, that I am the LORD. They will be my people, and I will be their God, for they will return to me with all their heart.

Lamentations 3:40

Let us examine our ways and test them, and let us return to the LORD.

Hosea 14:1-2

Return, Israel, to the LORD your God. Your sins have been your downfall!

[2] Take words with you and return to the LORD. Say to him: "Forgive all our sins and receive us graciously, that we may offer the fruit of our lips.

Of course, there are a multitude of other scriptures which could be referenced here as well. This message is repeated consistently throughout the Bible. The question is, will we truly examine ourselves from God's perspective (not our worldly perspective), and see how far we have wandered from Him? And when we find ourselves to be out of the Lord's will, will we humble ourselves, repent, and return to Him?

I think the book of Jonah would have happened differently if Jonah had made other choices. For example, if Jonah had done what God had asked in the first place, he would not have gotten on that ship. He would not have had to be tossed overboard in the storm. He would not have been swallowed by a great fish. And he would not have been vomited up by the fish (ewwwww). He didn't have to go through all that, but he did. Why? It wasn't God's choice for him. This was the ramifications of Jonah's decisions.

However, here is the grace and mercy of God. God could have easily allowed Jonah to die. Instead, God reached down to him and allowed a great fish to become a vehicle for Jonah. His own personal submarine, though not one I'd want to ride in. It was in the belly of the great fish that Jonah had his "come to Jesus" meeting.

A "come to Jesus" meeting is when we are confronted with our sins and are asked to repent. It is a point where we have to make up our minds. Are we going to surrender to God's desires for us or are we going to continue to try to fulfill our desires? The hope is that we "come to Jesus" and forsake our wayward ways.

Jonah's come to Jesus meeting came in the belly of the fish. Time was running out; he could not continue to exist as he had been. A real change needed to happen. The first place change happens is not outside of us but within us.

In chapter two of Jonah, we get to read about Jonah's prayer inside the belly of the fish. The entire prayer shares with us what Jonah has learned about the Lord, but in fact, it was what he had known about the Lord all along. All along Jonah knew that God was mighty, but more so, God preferred to show off His mercy. Those are two characteristics of God you can always count on. His mighty ability to do in the physical world what is beyond our comprehension. Secondly, His mercy can do what is beyond comprehension for our benefit, such as sending a great fish to be the vehicle for the salvation of Jonah. Or even greater, the fact that He would take someone who had gone against His desires back into His fold.

Even though Jonah had been defying God when Jonah turned to the Lord with his whole heart and surrendered to God, God quickly received him back into His fold. Isn't that an awesome God?!

God doesn't mind that often it is pain, discomfort, stress, uncertainty, fear, or something else that drives us to reach out to Him. God's desire is for us to learn and grow from our mistakes. To learn to trust in Him. To know that He is faithful and that He loves us in spite of our shortcomings.

His love for us, however, does not change His will for us. God did not say to Jonah, "Jonah, I know you don't want to go to Nineveh, so I've changed My will for you. I want you to go rest in a hot tub and just do whatever you feel like doing." God is God. God gets to make the decisions because He knows best. It's not God's job to get on board with our plans. It's our job to get on board with God's plans.

So if you are going through a storm or time of uncertainty, it's normal to meet God and draw even closer to Him during these times. God is OK with us running into His arms due to stress in our lives. God does not tell us to get our lives figured out then come to Him. He wants to help you get His direction for your life.

I thought God was leading my family across the country to Kentucky, but instead, he was leading us across town. In hindsight, it all makes perfect sense, but when I was going through it, my anxiety level was high. I was so scared of failing my family. I had informed our church, my district superintendent, and my friends from school that we were all set to go to Kentucky. I thought about all the bad judgment calls I had made earlier in my life and was nervous that this would turn out like some of those situations. Oh me of little faith.

As I tell this story, I just have to stop and praise God for a moment. Isn't God wonderful?! I was seeking to do His will and willing to pick up my family and move us to a new area, but it turned out that He was preparing to give me my heart's desire. He was moving me into full-time ministry at the place that fulfilled me the most, the Salina Rescue Mission. Thank you, God, for knowing how to give good gifts to your children!

CHAPTER 20

The Unveiling of God's Plan

As March was moving forward, I realized the doors weren't flying open the way we thought so I started asking God if perhaps He had other plans.

As I prayed for God's guidance I began to consider that perhaps it wasn't a church He was sending me to. Perhaps it was some other type of ministry. That's when it hit me. Maybe the Lord was leading me to a rescue mission in Kentucky. I remember being filled with joy at the thought.

I started doing some research online and was pleased to find three rescue missions in Kentucky. I thought with my volunteer experience perhaps one of them would be willing to give me an opportunity. So I started updating my resume and added my volunteer experience at the Salina Rescue Mission. I thought I would get a reference and an endorsement from the Salina Rescue Mission's Executive Director, Rev. Steve Kmetz.

I can't remember if I called Steve or sent him an email telling him about my plans of applying for a job at a rescue mission in Kentucky and asking if he would give me a letter of reference. Steve said, "Sure Chad. Of course, I would. However, I've got a crazy idea I'd like to run past you. Would you have time to have lunch with me one day?"

Could it be? Could he possibly be thinking of offering me a job? Could this be God opening a door He wanted me to walk through?

I shared it with my wife and she smiled. While we didn't know for sure that Steve was going to offer me a job, my wife affirmed she could easily see me working there and was very supportive of the opportunity. If in fact, that's what it was. So we prayed and asked God once again, to open the doors He wanted us to walk through and close the doors He didn't want us to walk through. Help us, Lord, to be in Your will.

As I met Steve for lunch, he shared with me that he was looking to retire sometime down the road and was looking for someone who could replace him one day. The Board had decided that they wanted to hire an Operations Director to learn to manage the Mission and potentially be someone he could groom to take his place when he retired.

I was excited about the possibility. Steve told me if I was interested to come by the Mission between certain hours to pick up an application. He asked me to return the application and resume during those same hours. I didn't know it then, but that was a test of his to see if I would follow instructions.

I did as Steve asked and was called in for an interview with Steve and one of the Board members, Ron. I don't remember if that was in April or May. All I knew was that we had to be out of the parsonage at the end of June, which was coming quick.

This was a little nerve-racking for Rene and I. Rene was thankful for the opportunity because even though she was willing to go to Kentucky for me, she desired to stay in Kansas close to her family. God is so good. He not only opened a door that I didn't even know I wanted, but He provided what my wife secretly desired too. Who says you can't have your cake and eat it too? God gave us our heart's deepest desires.

The timing felt a little chaotic because it was either the end of May or beginning of June when I was officially offered the job. We had to look for a home, but God provided that too. Every step of the way God answered our prayers faithfully in His time.

I have to confess, I would have liked to have had a road map of what was going to happen and when. I think we all get a little anxious not knowing what the outcomes are going to be. However, this is part of our spiritual journey of trusting that God is going to help us through it, one way or the other. The not knowing keeps us close to God and in the long run, enriches our lives. Plus, if there weren't any surprises in life, it would be boring. Life's far more exciting not knowing what God is about to do next.

One thing I have learned is that life with God is an awesome adventure. There are battles and times of peace. There are victories won and celebrations to be had. There are also times of sorrow where we are reminded that this world we live in is not the Heaven we are looking forward to.

God's provision of the ministry opportunity at the Salina Rescue Mission has been a rich blessing. When I came to work at the Mission, God gave me what I needed. I knew that I needed to sit under someone else's leadership and learn what it meant to be a leader. Steve has been a great mentor to me. He has challenged me to be sharpened as a leader and provided me with opportunities to grow along the way.

I'm not saying I've enjoyed all of the challenges, but God has certainly taught me a lot through them. That's the truth about God. He takes those tough times that we go through and turns them into life lessons, and we benefit from having gone through them.

My life of addiction and my selfishness in trying to live to please myself all the time was empty compared to the rich rewards of serving God and others. The Lord used those pains as part of His beautiful redemptive plan. He is now using me, with God's help and the help of everyone on our ministry team, to help other people who share in some of those same struggles.

As of this writing, I've been working at the Salina Rescue Mission for nine years now. Steve plans to retire, and the Board has decided that I will get the blessing of being the next Executive Director. God has been faithful all these years in slowly building me up. He's been teaching me and helping me learn how to teach others. It is to God's glory that He can use a broken person like me.

As I reflect on the journey, it's a time of remembering how faithful God has been. It's remembering what God has brought me out of and what God has brought me into.

My testimony is consistent with God's actions and words in the Bible. My story is similar to the story of Israel. Neither Israel, nor I, did things perfectly. We both fell to temptations, we strayed from the Lord, and at times outright rebelled against Him. Even though God could have easily wiped me off the face of the earth and given up on me, His mercy has prevailed.

Ephesians 2:1-9

**As for you, you were dead in your transgressions and sins, 2 in
which you used to live when you followed the ways of this world
and of the ruler of the kingdom of the air, the spirit who is now at
work in those who are disobedient. 3 All of us also lived among them
at one time, gratifying the cravings of our flesh and following its
desires and thoughts. Like the rest, we were by nature deserving
of wrath. 4 But because of his great love for us, God, who is rich
in mercy, 5 made us alive with Christ even when we were dead
in transgressions—it is by grace you have been saved. 6 And God
raised us up with Christ and seated us with him in the heavenly
realms in Christ Jesus, 7 in order that in the coming ages he might
show the incomparable riches of his grace, expressed in his
kindness to us in Christ Jesus. 8 For it is by grace you have been
saved, through faith—and this is not from yourselves, it is the gift
of God— 9 not by works, so that no one can boast.**

The Lord is teaching us something about being long-suffering. Long-suffering is something most of us do not do very well. In short, I understand it as giving a person second chances, and third chances, and more. The Lord's mercy and long-suffering is for OUR benefit, to give us all the opportunity to repent, to return to Him, and to find the glorious truth of His love and faithfulness.

God's plans for my life are better than the ones I had for myself. I used to want to be a rock-star. I wanted to have all the world had to offer. I wanted to indulge in all the desires of the flesh. But the truth is, that was an empty and painful attempt at me trying to live for myself.

It's only when I started living for God that He showed me a better and more fulfilling way to live. Since giving myself to the Lord I've moved from:

- Being unfulfilled with life, to having a life with meaning and purpose that is rewarding
- Being a man without a family, to having a wonderful wife and kids, and the joys that go with it
- Having a life of going from one wreck to the next, to peace and prosperity
- Being lost to helping the lost find their way
- Being a man without a home to having a home both here on earth, and an even better home awaiting in heaven

God knows how to give good gifts to those who love Him and are called according to His good purpose.

My encouragement for each of you is that you go on an adventure with God. Learn to give yourself fully to Him and see for yourself how good the Lord is.

Psalm 34:8

Taste and see that the LORD is good; blessed is the one who takes refuge in him.

CHAPTER 21

The Great Commission – The Son of Man Must Be Lifted Up

2 Corinthians 5:20

We are therefore Christ's ambassadors, as though God were making his appeal through us. We implore you on Christ's behalf: Be reconciled to God.

Sharing the gospel is not an act of judgment, or narrow-mindedness, as some try to make it. It is the truth we believe and an act of love. If I knew of something that could enrich your life, and I loved you, then it would only make sense that I would desire to share it with you.

John 3:12

12 I have spoken to you of earthly things and you do not believe; how then will you believe if I speak of heavenly things?

Here is the issue. Most of us start off struggling to understand the things of God. We try to make sense of God based on our human experience, but our sinful (self-serving) nature kicks in and wants to interpret the things of God in a way that serves our own desires. In essence, we want to be in control of God. We want to assign meaning to God (or the Atheist might say there is no God) so that we can live life according to our own set of rules. The truth is, even when we set our own rules for life, we often don't live up to them.

It's like Israel in the wilderness. In Exodus chapters 19-24, the Lord made a covenant (essentially an oath that would be considered a legal binding agreement in today's terms) with Israel and gave them the Ten Commandments. The people all agreed to live by the commandments of the Lord.

The first two commandments are:

Exodus 20:2-6

2 "I am the LORD your God, who brought you out of Egypt, out of the land of slavery.

3 "You shall have no other gods before me.

4 "You shall not make for yourself an image in the form of anything in heaven above or on the earth beneath or in the waters below. 5 You shall not bow down to them or worship them; for I, the LORD your God, am a jealous God, punishing the children for the sin of the parents to the third and fourth generation of those who hate me, 6 but showing love to a thousand generations of those who love me and keep my commandments.

To put this in context, God is in the process of revealing Himself to Israel. He is helping them know Him at a deeper, more personal level. He wants to be known by them. He desires to live in relationship with them. He just rescued them from Egypt and gave ten miraculous signs that His favor was upon them. Despite the might of Pharaoh, God was stronger than all of Egypt and was willing and able to intervene on their behalf.

He revealed Himself as a loving God desiring the best for Israel as He delivered them from Egypt and slavery. He delivered them not only from slavery but delivered them with a plan to give them a land of their own, a fertile land that is described as a land of milk and honey (Exodus 3:8, 3:17, 13:5, and 33:3).

God starts off the Ten Commandments by reminding them of what He has already done for them. If nothing else, they should love and accept Him for what He has already done. He has proven Himself to be worthy of being first in their lives and worthy of being their One and only God in a culture where people had a myriad of gods for every occasion.

The second commandment says not to give in to the temptation to make other gods alongside God, for the Lord God is jealous for you. The temptation is to think that God is not enough for you. The temptation is to give the love and devotion that belongs to God to others, and that is just not acceptable to God.

If you meditate upon what God is telling us, He is saying that He has an area in His heart where He is vulnerable. He has a weakness, and it's His love and commitment to you. He is jealous for you. He loves you so deeply that it hurts His heart to consider you may reject Him.

God shares that our rejection of Him will have a devastating effect on us. The consequences we will bring upon ourselves for rejecting Him will impact not only us but our children, and our children's children. And that's not a threat. It's a loving warning. It is God saying to us, don't touch the stove or you will burn yourself. Only here, God is saying there is so much more on the line.

God is appealing to us to consider the decisions we need to make about our relationship with Him. How we choose to live our lives affects not only ourselves but the decisions we make also affect our children and our grandchildren. If we don't care so much about what happens to us, then He, our great Heavenly Father, is begging us to consider how our decisions will affect those we love the most.

God as a Father knows what it is to deeply love His children and desire the best for them. He desires to share with us the blessings life has to offer. God is crying out for us to take our most cherished, our children, and consider how our relationship with God can impact them, both in the positive and the negative.

Then He, with His true desire, joyfully tells us that the greatness of His love spans to a thousand generations!!!!! He begs us to choose the better things in life. To choose to have a relationship with Him that is able to bless you and your beloved children to a thousand generations. To us this is unimaginable, it's almost inconceivable.

Isaiah 64:4-5

Since ancient times no one has heard, no ear has perceived, no eye has seen any God besides you, who acts on behalf of those who wait for him. [5] You come to the help of those who gladly do right, who remember your ways.

Too often people have read these first two commandments without considering the heart of God and what it is He is trying to communicate to us. He is essentially saying we can trust Him because He has already acted on our behalf. And if we will wholeheartedly give ourselves to Him, He joyfully gives Himself to us.

Throughout God's Word, we read of a person after person having a human experience with a Heavenly God. Unfortunately, many of us try to make sense of it without knowing who God really is. Without knowing how deep His love is for us or how richly He desires to bless us throughout our lives.

We live life, trying to figure it out without knowing or understanding our Creator God who has a plan and a purpose for our lives. If only we would seek Him.

So God gave Israel these two commandments (followed by eight more). Soon afterward Moses goes up the mountain to spend time close to God, seeking God's guidance and direction to lead God's people to the Promised Land. After Moses disappears what do the people do? They create their own god.

They make a calf out of the gold they had brought with them out of Egypt. In Exodus 32 you can read the full story.

Essentially, they had relied on Moses' relationship with God to guide them. They had not taken to heart what God's first two commandments were. They were to have a personal relationship with the Lord. They were to serve Him with love, adoration, faithfulness, joy and devotion. They said yes to the Covenant but they had not fully given their hearts to the Lord, which is what He was asking for. To add insult to injury, they gave this golden calf the credit for what God had done.

When we don't know the Lord, we fall to the temptation of wanting to place ourselves in control. We want to trust in our own worldly wisdom. We don't want to trust God because we never take the time to understand Him and His love for us.

There were drastic consequences, but that was not God's desire. The people chose to act in defiance of what God had commanded them, direct defiance. It was their way of killing God and throwing Him away. They had chosen to be enemies of God through their disobedience.

This disobedience, this shameful way we have treated God, is something we don't want to acknowledge or look at. Instead of us accepting responsibility for the situation we create, we want to ask God to forgive and pretend that it never happened.

God cannot be unjust if He is to reign. If God's Kingdom is to be one of peace, holiness, and righteousness, then He cannot allow sin to continue in His Kingdom. Otherwise, you would have chaos.

Consider this, what if our government, our law-makers, were to say stealing is illegal (which, of course, it is). Then when someone stole something, instead of giving them consequences for their action they had a policy that they were going to forgive every crime with no punishment at all. So the person with a drug addiction who needed more money could easily go out and steal and not have to face any consequences. How safe would our society be?

The truth is we need laws, and consequences, for our society to have any chance of making it. This is both an earthly and spiritual lesson.

John 3:13-15

13 No one has ever gone into heaven except the one who came from
heaven—the Son of Man. 14 Just as Moses lifted up the snake in the
wilderness, so the Son of Man must be lifted up, 15 that everyone
who believes may have eternal life in him."

As Moses lifted up the snake in the wilderness...

Numbers 21:4-9

4 They traveled from Mount Hor along the route to the Red Sea,
to go around Edom. But the people grew impatient on the way; 5
they spoke against God and against Moses, and said, "Why have
you brought us up out of Egypt to die in the wilderness? There
is no bread! There is no water! And we detest this miserable
food!"

6 Then the LORD sent venomous snakes among them; they bit the
people and many Israelites died. 7 The people came to Moses and
said, "We sinned when we spoke against the LORD and against
you. Pray that the LORD will take the snakes away from us." So
Moses prayed for the people.

8 The LORD said to Moses, "Make a snake and put it up on a pole;
anyone who is bitten can look at it and live." 9 So Moses made a
bronze snake and put it up on a pole. Then when anyone was
bitten by a snake and looked at the bronze snake, they lived.

Jesus is telling us that the bronze snake lifted up by Moses in the wilderness is the same reason why Jesus was here on earth as a human being. He was here to be hung upon the cross so that we may look to Him to be saved.

Consider this.

Israel was complaining about God and Moses because, in their eyes, they didn't do enough for them. Previously the people were complaining of having no food, so God sent manna, bread from Heaven to feed them. The Lord showed Himself to be their provider. God proved through His actions that He would make sure they had what they needed.

Human beings are interesting, to say the least. In this case, the people begged for food. God gave them manna to feed them, and they rejoiced. Now they have had the manna for years (the Bible says that they ate manna for 40 years until they entered the Promised Land), and the thankfulness has disappeared, and the complaining has begun, again.

God blessed them with bread from heaven, but they wanted more. They wanted pot roast, lasagna, steak and potatoes (in more common terms of course). It wasn't enough to have a steady flow of God's miraculous provision, faithfully for decades. No, they wanted to tell God how to do the miracles. They essentially were treating God like their personal chef saying they were going to fire Him if He didn't fix them something else to eat.

Do these folks know how to insult God or what?

How could God allow such a people to inherit the great blessing He plans to give them? If He does what can we expect they will do once they get there? My guess is to complain more and continue to ask God to be their servant.

God sent the serpents to remind Israel that He was God and not to be taken lightly. The people getting bitten by the poisonous snake is God's reminder to the people of what had happened in the Garden of Eden. The serpent had sown the seed of thought to Eve that she didn't need God, that she could know what was best on her own. She could prove it by defying God and eating of the Tree of Knowledge of Good and Evil.

That serpent got his poison in the bloodline of humanity, and we have been falling to that same sinful thought ever since. The snake bite was a message to those people, and to us. When we start treating God like He is short-changing us, that is sin rearing its ugly head in our hearts.

Moses prayed for the people and appealed to God to show mercy to them. God's plan of mercy was revealed. He tells Moses to take the image of the snake and hang it on a tall pole, to cast it in bronze and hang it high so all the people can see it and be saved.

Hanging the snake on the pole is the foretelling of God's plan of salvation for all of humanity through the crucifixion of Jesus on the cross. The snake represented the sins of the people. If the people would acknowledge their sin and look upon the bronze snake on the pole, they would be saved from death.

Jesus tells us that He is going to fulfill this in His death on the cross. Jesus is going to bear our sins and allow Himself to be crucified so that we can be set free from the penalty of sin.

John 3:16-17

16 For God so loved the world that he gave his one and only Son, that whoever believes in him shall not perish but have eternal life. 17 For God did not send his Son into the world to condemn the world, but to save the world through him.

This is the Good News, the Gospel. All you have to do is be willing to believe in Jesus. Believe Jesus is the Son of God, sent here to pay the price for your sins so that you can be reunited with God in heaven.

God did this for us. He did for us what we could not do for ourselves.

John 3:18-21

18 Whoever believes in him is not condemned, but whoever does
not believe stands condemned already because they have not
believed in the name of God's one and only Son. 19 This is the
verdict: Light has come into the world, but people loved darkness
instead of light because their deeds were evil. 20 Everyone who
does evil hates the light, and will not come into the light for fear
that their deeds will be exposed. 21 But whoever lives by the truth
comes into the light, so that it may be seen plainly that what they
have done has been done in the sight of God.

Here is the uncomfortable truth. Not everyone will be saved. Why? Because not everyone is willing to put their faith in Jesus and accept that He is their Savior. When Moses told the Israelites that if they got bit by a snake all they had to do was look to the pole with the bronze serpent and they would be saved. I am willing to bet that there were people that thought that was a bunch of nonsense and refused to look at the pole. I bet many died in their stubbornness.

When will we learn to humbly accept what God has done for us and realize the only real way to live rightly in God's creation is to live as God desires us to live? God desires good things for us. God wants us to enjoy life and all of creation. But there is clearly a right way to enjoy what God has created and a way to abuse the privileges we have been given.

This leads us each to a moment of decision. What will you do with this information? Are you going to receive it and learn to walk closely with the Lord? Or are you going to write it off and go on living on your own terms?

CHAPTER 22

Whom Will You Serve

Joshua 24:14-15

"Now fear the LORD and serve him with all faithfulness. Throw away the gods your ancestors worshiped beyond the Euphrates River and in Egypt, and serve the LORD. [15] But if serving the LORD seems undesirable to you, then choose for yourselves this day whom you will serve, whether the gods your ancestors served beyond the Euphrates, or the gods of the Amorites, in whose land you are living. But as for me and my household, we will serve the LORD."

We each need to make a decision about whether or not we will choose to receive what the Lord has done for us. My decision is not one I made fifteen years ago; it is a decision I make daily, as I choose to put Jesus on the throne of my life.

This world is filled with a variety of religious views, philosophies, and half-truths. It gets confusing as we begin to walk into the realm of spiritual matters. It's not something one can do in a day, week or month. It takes time to walk through the issues, the questions, and the misconceptions we have. We have biases we have to acknowledge and come to terms with. Quite frankly, it is a lot of work to walk through the muck and mire to come to a good understanding of what you believe and why.

Over the years, since I have given my life to Christ, I continue to grow in faith and understanding. I believe more today than I did fifteen years ago because of my experience and transformation in walking with God. I have seen God's presence actively at work in my life. There is a reason my faith is growing.

I once had a conversation with a dear friend who said he just couldn't walk in blind faith. I shared with him faith is not empty or hollow and from where I stand today, it is not blind. Faith means knowing what you believe in. Or in this case, Who you have faith in. We grow in faith through knowledge from the Bible and our life experiences with God.

The people of Israel had seen God perform the miracles of the plagues in Egypt. They saw Him part the Red Sea. They saw Him provide water from a rock. They ate the manna from heaven. Many still grumbled and complained and some even continued to question whether or not God's plan was right for them.

Consider any of the many blind men that were healed by Jesus. I'm sure the moment their eyesight returned was full of great joy, and at that moment, they believed.

I want to bring forward the story of one blind man's healing in particular. It's found in the Gospel According to John.

John 9:1-41

As he went along, he saw a man blind from birth. [2] His disciples asked him, "Rabbi, who sinned, this man or his parents, that he was born blind?"

[3] "Neither this man nor his parents sinned," said Jesus, "but this happened so that the works of God might be displayed in him. [4] As long as it is day, we must do the works of him who sent me. Night is coming, when no one can work. [5] While I am in the world, I am the light of the world."

[6] After saying this, he spit on the ground, made some mud with the saliva, and put it on the man's eyes. [7] "Go," he told him, "wash in the Pool of Siloam" (this word means "Sent"). So the man went and washed, and came home seeing.

[8] His neighbors and those who had formerly seen him begging asked, "Isn't this the same man who used to sit and beg?" [9] Some claimed that he was.

Others said, "No, he only looks like him."

But he himself insisted, "I am the man."

[10] "How then were your eyes opened?" they asked.

[11] He replied, "The man they call Jesus made some mud and put it on my eyes. He told me to go to Siloam and wash. So I went and washed, and then I could see."

[12] "Where is this man?" they asked him.

"I don't know," he said.

The Pharisees Investigate the Healing

[13] They brought to the Pharisees the man who had been blind. [14] Now the day on which Jesus had made the mud and opened the man's eyes was a Sabbath.[15] Therefore, the Pharisees also asked him how he had received his sight. "He put mud on my eyes," the man replied, "and I washed, and now I see."

[16] Some of the Pharisees said, "This man is not from God, for he does not keep the Sabbath."

But others asked, "How can a sinner perform such signs?" So they were divided.

[17] Then they turned again to the blind man, "What have you to say about him? It was your eyes he opened."

The man replied, "He is a prophet."

[18] They still did not believe that he had been blind and had received his sight until they sent for the man's parents. [19] "Is this your son?" they asked. "Is this the one you say was born blind? How is it that now he can see?"

[20] "We know he is our son," the parents answered, "and we know he was born blind. [21] But how he can see now, or who opened his eyes, we don't know. Ask him. He is of age; he will speak for himself." [22] His parents said this because they were afraid of the Jewish leaders, who already had decided that anyone who acknowledged that Jesus was the Messiah would be put out of the synagogue. [23] That was why his parents said, "He is of age; ask him."

[24] A second time they summoned the man who had been blind. "Give glory to God by telling the truth," they said. "We know this man is a sinner."

[25] He replied, "Whether he is a sinner or not, I don't know. One thing I do know. I was blind but now I see!"

[26] Then they asked him, "What did he do to you? How did he open your eyes?"

[27] He answered, "I have told you already and you did not listen. Why do you want to hear it again? Do you want to become his disciples too?"

[28] Then they hurled insults at him and said, "You are this fellow's disciple! We are disciples of Moses! [29] We know that God spoke to Moses, but as for this fellow, we don't even know where he comes from."

[30] The man answered, "Now that is remarkable! You don't know where he comes from, yet he opened my eyes. [31] We know that God does not listen to sinners. He listens to the godly person who does his will. [32] Nobody has ever heard of opening the eyes of a man born blind. [33] If this man were not from God, he could do nothing."

[34] To this they replied, "You were steeped in sin at birth; how dare you lecture us!" And they threw him out.

Spiritual Blindness

[35] Jesus heard that they had thrown him out, and when he found him, he said, "Do you believe in the Son of Man?"

[36] "Who is he, sir?" the man asked. "Tell me so that I may believe in him."

[37] Jesus said, "You have now seen him; in fact, he is the one speaking with you."

[38] Then the man said, "Lord, I believe," and he worshiped him.

[39] Jesus said, "For judgment I have come into this world, so that the blind will see and those who see will become blind."

[40] Some Pharisees who were with him heard him say this and asked, "What? Are we blind too?"

[41] Jesus said, "If you were blind, you would not be guilty of sin; but now that you claim you can see, your guilt remains.

The blind man received his healing because he acted on faith by doing what Jesus asked him to do, to wash his eyes in the Pool of Siloam. He doesn't know how Jesus healed him, only that Jesus did it. The man started by acting on what little faith he had, and because of the healing the man walked away believing all the more.

The man could not deny what happened to him. I was blind, now I see.

That's my testimony also. I heard of Jesus but didn't know Him. I came to meet Jesus to decide for myself. Somewhere in this journey, I started trusting Jesus and acting upon that trust. The facts are undeniable; Jesus changed my life. He saved me from my life of pain and self-loathing and has given me a wonderful, fulfilling life.

I don't fully understand it all. All I know is He rescued me and gave me a life I'm very happy to have. Things aren't perfect, but they're a lot better. I'm not perfect, but I am a lot better, to His credit, praise, and glory.

I'm an imperfect Christian living in an imperfect world, but I do not allow that to become an excuse for being less than what Jesus wants me to be. Nor am I using the imperfection within me, or this world, to become an excuse to live according to the ways of the world.

It's in following Jesus, and doing my best to be obedient to Him, that He has given me a miracle. He made something out of my life when I could not make anything of it on my own. All honor and glory rightly belongs to Jesus, and I will follow Him all of my days, to the best of my ability. Prayerfully, I'll continue to decrease and He will continue to increase in me.

If you desire to get to know Jesus and experience a miraculous change in yourself, start by choosing to surrender your life to His care, on a daily basis.

Here is my invitation to you. Seven steps to take to grow your faith:

The 1st step – Come and follow Jesus. – Seek Him. Get to know Jesus by reading the four gospels (Matthew, Mark, Luke, and John). Learn what He teaches, how He loves, who He loves, and what His desires are for us in this world.

The 2nd step – Continue to learn His ways and grow with Him. Jesus did not reveal Himself fully to me in a day, a week, or a month. The more time you spend with Jesus, the better you will come to know and understand Him. Invest some time with Him; it's well worth the investment. Spend time with Him while reading the Bible and pray to God to help you understand.

Find a church where you can feel free to ask questions and seek answers. This is an important part of spiritual development. God teaches us a lot of lessons as we live in relationship with one another.

The 3rd step – Who do you say I am? – At some point in this journey, and maybe at several points, you need to be able to answer the question of who Jesus is to you.

The 4th step – Surrender your life to Him. We are not to live as Christians in name only and in all other ways to resemble the world. The Lord will call for your loyalty and ask you to make some changes in your life. The Lord will lead you to serve others and make a difference in the world in His name. You will grow tremendously as you do this. You will also reap the rewards of joy and peace as you fulfill your purpose.

The 5th step – Share Him with others – not as judgment or condemnation – but as a wonderful gift. The only way we come to know Jesus is because others were faithful in carrying the message to us. Do your part, as an act of love, and share the forgiveness and love of God with others.

The 6th step – Live in such a way as you are awaiting His return. Your testimony will be either brightened or dulled by how you live out your faith. The Bible calls us to live as if Christ could return at any moment. When Christ returns desire to be found being faithful to Him.

The 7th step – Rest in Him. Receive the peace and joy of having your salvation and life secure in Christ. Resting does not mean you don't need to keep growing. Once you have committed your life to Him you will come to understand that we need to continue growing in faith and understanding throughout the entirety of our lives.

I encourage you to get involved in a church family. Know this, church families, like real families, are not perfect. They are made up of imperfect people who are all at different stages in their journeys of faith. Others can help you on this journey. You will need their support at times and they will need your support at times.

Make sure the Bible is your final source of authority. If people are teaching things that are contradictory to the Bible, find a new group of people to associate with. Be careful that the herd you are running with aren't heading for a cliff.

May you find the rich rewards of having a living, and active, relationship with the Lord Jesus Christ! May the Lord bless and enrich your life.

Works Cited

Adams, Jay E. *A Theology of Christian Counseling: More Than Redemption.* Grand Rapids: Zondervan Publishing House, 1979.

McGee, Robert S. *The Search for Significance.* Nashville: W Publishing Group, 1998.

Miller, J. Keith. *A Hunger for Healing: The Twelve Steps as a Classic Model for Christian Spiritual Growth.* New York: HarperCollins, 1991.

New International Version. *Biblegateway.com.* n.d. 1-31 January - June 2016.

Patterson, C. Michael. *www.credohouse.org.* 22 June 2015. 21 June 2016. <http://credohouse.org/blog/what-happened-to-the-twelve-apostles-how-do-their-deaths-prove-easter>.